"She has finally done it, and I am so excited for my friend of over twenty-five years—Martha Munizzi—to share it. I have watched her influence our world and the faith of believers through her powerful music. I personally have heard stories of her impact on every continent. *Because of Who You Are* is full of transparent personal stories that will encourage you, lift your spirit, and give you hope for the future!"
—Dr. Dave Martin, Success Coach, Author, and Pastor

"Worship is powerful. God uses worship to lift us higher and to make our perspective more like His own. In *Because of Who You Are*, Martha Munizzi takes readers on a journey through some of the most impactful worship songs she's written. You'll be revived and challenged, and you'll gain a deeper appreciation of worship!"
—Martijn van Tilborgh, Founder of Four Rivers Media

"When I think of Martha Munizzi, I think of words like 'faithfulness, brave, gifted, anointed, selfless, generous' . . . and my list goes on and on. And what I know about this book, is that it will be a GREAT encouragement to all who read it as Martha pours out her heart to bring personal testament to the goodness of God over such a beautiful, worshipful life journey. THANK YOU Martha for your Romans 12 life. I am so thankful to God for your life and the way you continue to shine for the glory of God."
—Darlene Zschech, Award-Winning Recording Artist,
Co-Pastor Hope Unlimited Church, NSW, Australia

"There are difficult moments in life where words fail. I remember when my husband Steve had a massive heart attack and was dying in front of me. I couldn't think of a single prayer to pray or a song to sing. My sister Martha was my first call in the middle of that trauma and she kept me anchored in hope. All I could do was sing Martha's song, 'Say the Name of Jesus.' This song is one of the most powerful songs my sister has ever written and from personal experience, it has a healing anointing on it. You need to read this book to find out the end of my story as well as read more stories of my sister's life that will encourage you, challenge you, and bring you hope!"

—Mary Alessi, Singer/Songwriter/Author,
Co-Pastor Metro Life Church, Miami, FL

"The secret to being a great artist, singer, and songwriter is not limited to their ability to sing but to tell a story through music that impacts people's lives. For decades, Martha Munizzi has not only written countless 'hits' with her music but has also impacted millions with her message of hope and transformation. In her new book, *Because of Who You Are*, you will read the powerful, hope-filled stories behind the lyrics. They will change how you live."

—Rodney and Michelle Gage, Authors, Speakers,
and Pastors of ReThink Life Church

"*Because of Who You Are* is not a typical book. Each chapter particularizes why Martha wrote her songs and how the Holy Spirit directed her. Martha compels her readers to experience her life's journey in a manner that creates expectancy and anticipation at the outcome of her stories. Each chapter captures the DNA of her music and the 'why' it was written.

While reading *Because of Who You Are*, I couldn't help but be reminded of how King David was inspired to write precious songs of worship to the Lord from the space of his betrayals, sin, failures, and victories. In that manner, Martha's stories about her children, her ministry, her husband, and her spiritual journey led to her writing some of the greatest gospel music in the Kingdom. I appreciate Martha's unfiltered voice in this book. Her stories are transparent and remarkably genuine.

This compilation of Martha's vivid testimonies will vastly increase her readers' faith and allow them to enter a realm of life-changing worship."

—Dr. Riva Watkins, Pastor/Author,
Majestic Life Church, Orlando, FL

"If you want to know why there is such a power and anointing in Martha Munizzi's songs, read through these stories, and you'll know why! More than just a melody and lyrics, her songs are filled with a revelation from God's Word, birthed from deeply personal experiences and prayer. Powerful!"

—Don Moen, Award-Winning Recording
Artist & Songwriter, Nashville, TN

"Martha Munizzi has been leading worship and writing worship music for decades. There are few people who understand the approach to the throne any better or can write the language for a generation of people to sing along and follow her on the path into God's presence. Now she's taken us even further with the book you hold in your hand—*Because of Who You Are*—by telling us her personal stories that inspired the anthems that churches all over the world are singing. Martha is an amazing worshiper and an even greater communicator. Be inspired by her journey."

—David Binion, Singer/Songwriter/Author,
Lead Pastor, Dwell Church, Dallas, TX

"Martha Munizzi's gift for songwriting has always been clearly evident in the amazing songs she has written. Not only does this book clearly re-iterate that fact, but it also reminds me, all over again, of her passion for worship, and for ministering to the body of Christ. Every story, every lyric, every example in this book, is like a B-12 shot to the spirit man in all of us. I just want to say thank you, Martha, for being so transparent, and allowing your journey to be an inspiration to all of us! So powerful!!"

—Geron Davis, Award-Winning Recording
Artist & Songwriter, Nashville, TN

"This book encourages, inspires, and challenges me as a worship leader and songwriter. I couldn't help but sense the presence of the Lord while reading it. Every chapter gives me an inside look at the journey and history of someone that has walked so closely with Jesus and has made such an impact on the world as a result. It's evidence that God is good all the time! These are not just stories and songs, they are testimonies. I believe Martha is one of the greatest worship leaders and songwriters of our generation, and her life is an example of humility, purity, and pursuit of The Lord. Reading her book will undoubtedly charge you with faith and a greater passion for the Lord!"

—John Wilds, Singer/Songwriter, Bethel Music,
Worship Pastor Calvary Christian Center, Ormond Beach, FL

"I've known Martha for many years, and her passion for leading people into the presence of God has never wavered. Her new book chronicles the crafting of that passion into many of the songs featured on her Award Winning Record, 'The Best Is Yet To Come.' The ability to peek behind the curtain and see the process allows us to glean from the many encounters Martha and her team experienced during the creation of this body of work. And as you read each chapter, I also believe that fresh encounters await you."

—Da'dra Greathouse, Worship Leader,
Lakewood Church, Houston, TX

BECAUSE OF WHO
YOU ARE

THE STORIES BEHIND MY MUSIC

MARTHA MUNIZZI

ARROWS &
STONES

This book is dedicated to my amazing husband, Dan, who has been a constant source of strength and encouragement in my life. I love you.

To my three children, Danielle, Nicole and Nathan, I love you all so much. I am so blessed to be your mom.

And to my mother, Faith, who taught me how to trust Jesus. I love you.

CONTENTS

♪

INTRODUCTION

I love stories! Stories are powerful! A great story can move someone, change their mind, impact them, make a powerful point, and provoke thought.

Stories appeal to our senses and our emotions. Stories are more powerful than facts and are actually remembered up to 22 times more than facts alone, according to Stanford professor Jennifer Aaker. So if you share a story, you can persuade someone more quickly than data, facts, and figures can.

Stories have shaped my life. Whether it was powerful, funny, life-altering, tragic, or humiliating—more times than I can count—a story has changed my perspective and caused me to see things differently. My late father was a great songwriter, preacher, and master storyteller. He had an amazing sense of humor and could remember and recite every joke he had ever heard. My late father-in-law, an Italian immigrant, could bring tears to your eyes with his stories of how hard it was being bullied as a-nine-year old boy in America who couldn't speak English. Then, a few minutes later, he would turn our tears into laughter with one of his stories about his many comical on-the-job experiences as a building contractor. Both of these men could keep an audience begging to tell the same story they had heard

xii BECAUSE OF WHO YOU ARE

a hundred times or more. Although the stories became a little more embellished each time they told them, no one seemed to mind.

Stories reveal and teach us a lot about ourselves. We can be moved by a powerful story, impacted enough to give to an important cause, motivated to change the course of our life, or inspired to become more than we ever imagined!

> *Stories reveal and teach us a lot about ourselves. We can be moved by a powerful story, impacted enough to give to an important cause, motivated to change the course of our life, or inspired to become more than we ever imagined!*

Not only do I love to hear a great story, but I also love to tell stories. I've been told I'm a good storyteller, and over the years, I've worked on getting better at sharing my life experiences by crafting stories from situations I've actually gone through. This book is a compilation of real and raw life situations I've encountered as well as the true stories behind thirty-one of the songs I've written. There are a few stories in this book in which I've chosen to omit or change people's names to protect the innocent and not incriminate anyone (smile); however, all of the stories are true.

My hope and prayer is that as you read this book, you will be impacted, motivated, inspired, and enlightened. I really hope you see yourself in the stories, laugh a little, and relate to them. I pray that your love and desire for Jesus and His presence will grow. Through these stories, scriptures, and lyrics of my songs, be encouraged and uplifted.

ONE

BECAUSE OF WHO YOU ARE

♪

*Because of who You are,
I give You glory
Because of who You are,
I give You praise
Because of who You are,
I will lift my voice and say
Lord, I worship You because
of who You are
Lord, I worship You because
of who You are*

*Jehovah Jireh, my provider
Jehovah Nissi, Lord,
You reign in victory
Jehovah Shalom, my
Prince of Peace
And I worship You because
of who You are*

MUSIC AND LYRICS BY MARTHA MUNIZZI & DAN MUNIZZI

I wrote this song several years ago while I was getting my kids ready for bed. One night—it was a normal, ordinary moment—we were doing something we did every night after a day of playing outside and running in the yard without shoes on like all kids do. The kids were dirty and sweaty, so they were all in the bathtub. I was sitting there thinking how grateful I was to be their mother. It was a chaotic moment of kids splashing, laughing and trying to dunk each other—and me desperately wanting them to just get out, grab their towels, dry off without fighting, get their SpongeBob or Strawberry Shortcake pajamas on, and get into bed. But God interrupted that very ordinary, mundane moment and whispered the melody and lyrics into my heart for "Because of Who You Are."

Because of who You are I give You glory.
Because of who You are I give You praise.

And in one millisecond, I knew the Holy Spirit had given me a gift. I knew this song was a download from heaven. So I hurried to get my kids into bed, and I called my mother to sing it to her. I said, "Mom, I wrote this song. And the chorus says that we worship God for who He is . . . but who is He?"

"Well," my mother said, "the Bible says He's *Jehovah Jireh*, which means He's our provider. And He's *Jehovah Nissi*—our banner of victory."

I spent the rest of the night studying the names of God, and I finished the song. And if you had asked me when I wrote the song if I thought it would be sung all over the world, I would've said, "No way," because I had no idea the gift God had given me in this song. And while I was thanking Him for the gift of my children and reflecting on how blessed I was to be their mom, God downloaded a gift into my spirit: a song that eventually blessed and encouraged His children all over the world. In other words, my thanksgiving released the blessing of God in that moment.

You know, the older I get, the more I realize God is never trying to just bless *me*. It's never just about encouraging *me* and making sure all *my* needs are met. The truth is I'm blessed to be a blessing. God encourages me, so I can encourage others. He counsels, heals, challenges, and pours into me. He disciples me, so I can do all those things for those around me. It's always so much bigger than I am!

The truth is I'm blessed to be a blessing. God encourages me, so I can encourage others. He counsels, heals, challenges, and pours into me. He disciples me, so I can do all those things for those around me. It's always so much bigger than I am.

The Bible says He's our healer. God is our way-maker. He's our rock. He is *Jehovah Jireh*, our provider. He's *Jehovah Nissi*, our victory. He's *Jehovah Shalom*, our peace. And we worship Him for more than what He's done or will ever do for us. True worship is thanking God for who He is. Philippians 4:19 (NLT) tells us, "This same God who takes care of me will supply all your needs from His glorious riches, which have been given to us in Christ Jesus." Paul was saying, "This same God who provided for me will provide for you."

God reveals Himself to us through His many different names in the Bible. There is not one single name that could ever describe all God is. God uses each and every one of His names to reveal a different part of His character to us. Each name has significance. I encourage you as you're praying, worshiping God, and going about your day to begin to thank God for who He is. He is your provider! If you have a need, God's Word promises that need is provided for. If you need victory in your life, you serve *Jehovah Nissi*, the God who is our victory. If you need peace in your life, thank Him that He is *Jehovah Shalom*. Worship God for more than just what He has done or will ever do for you. Worship God, and thank Him for who He is!

Scan to download the song from this chapter.

PRAYER

Lord, I thank You for who You are. You are Jehovah Jireh—You provide every need I have. Your name is Jehovah Nissi—You are my victory. Your name is all-powerful and mighty, and at the name of Jesus demons flee. I praise You for more than what You've done for me—I praise You because of who You are! You are my rock, my fortress, and my strong tower. You are my help, my healer, my deliverer, and my strength. Today, I will worship You with everything I have because You are worthy, and You deserve all of my praise! In Jesus's name. Amen!

TWO

'TIL THE WALLS FALL

♪

You are awesome, God
You are mighty King
You're my sword and shield
You are my strength

In this one thing
I am confident
You will fight for me
You are my defense

I will not back up, not
   back down
Stake my claim, stand
   my ground
Shout for joy 'til the
   walls fall down

And I will praise until
   the walls fall
'Til the chains break
Praise until the enemy's
   under my feet

Praise until the walls fall
'Til the chains break
Praise until the walls fall down
Praise until the walls fall
Praise until the enemy's
   under my feet
Praise until the walls fall
I will stand my ground 'til
   the walls fall down
I will not be defeated
I will not be destroyed
Praise is the weapon
But the battle is the Lord's

I will not back up, not
   back down
Stake my claim, stand
   my ground
Shout for joy 'til the
   walls fall down

MUSIC AND LYRICS BY MARTHA MUNIZZI

Walls are barriers. Barriers are obstacles that stand in your way and prevent forward movement or access to your desired location. What wall or barrier is preventing your movement or access, keeping you stagnant, and maybe even paralyzing you from moving into the good things God has for you: a better job, a healthier relationship, or greater faith? Barriers can be resentment, unforgiveness, anger, or rejection that you face on a daily basis.

Praising God every day will shift your focus off of your problems and onto the ability that only God has. Praise is a spiritual weapon that we have as believers that will remove the walls and barriers that are in your way, preventing you from moving forward. When you declare daily that God is awesome, that He's the mighty King, that He's your sword and shield, and that He is your strength, you will begin to develop confidence in the strength and the ability of God's power in your life. God's thoughts are higher than your thoughts. God's ways are higher than your ways. Renew your mind daily with God's Word, and replace thoughts of defeat with the truth of who God is. God promises us in His word that He is able to do more than anything you could ever ask or think.

> *When you declare daily that God is awesome, that He's the mighty King, that He's your sword and shield, and that He is your strength, you will begin to develop confidence in the strength and the ability of God's power.*

Now, if I'm being honest, there have been days that I have been tempted to think about and rehash all the negative things that have happened in my life. Years ago, if someone had hurt my feelings or offended me, I would literally have spent days focused on what the offending party had said. I would wish that I had said something in response to what they said. I would spend additional time thinking about the problem or the person who hurt me and only end up more angry and resentful.

I've had to learn to stop focusing on what I can't control and trust God to be my defense. It's way too easy to focus on what you can't control, to obsess about what you don't have, or to dwell on a problem for way too long until you've blown it out of proportion. You'll cause yourself to become increasingly upset over something you never should have even worried about in the first place. Then, you open the door for the enemy to amplify your problems even more.

There's so much power when you praise! When you exalt God, He will give you strategies, insights, discernment, and direction. He will show you how to demolish the walls and the barriers that are standing in the way and restricting you from moving forward into forgiveness and freedom. God will show you areas in your life that aren't surrendered to Him so that you can walk in greater freedom. The truth is that every obstacle has already been defeated, and you already have the victory. If the enemy tries to use your insecurities to torment you, you don't have to listen to his lies. Don't shrink back in fear. Don't miss out on the miracle God has for your life. Joy is a praise away!

God said in Deuteronomy 7:16 (NKJV), "You shall destroy all the peoples whom the Lord your God delivers over to you; your eye shall have no pity on them; nor shall you serve their gods, for that will be a snare to you." This is important because there are snares in our lives that God tells us in His Word that we are to "have no pity on" and must destroy. What are the snares in your life? What is hindering you from accessing all that God has for you? Could it be a past relationship that you haven't let go of? Could it be something in your life that God wants to reconcile—a relationship, maybe something you haven't forgiven yourself or someone else for? Could it be that anger, resentment, or a lack of confidence has become a snare?

Victory is a shout away. Joshua 6:20 says that at the sound of the trumpet, when the Israelite army gave a loud shout, the walls collapsed. Everyone charged straight in, and they took the city. They devoted the city to the Lord and destroyed with the sword every living thing in it—men and women, young and old, cattle, sheep, and donkeys. A shout of praise is a weapon of spiritual warfare, and when we face walls in our lives, we need to give a shout of victory in order to see the walls fall! If the Israelites had not shouted, the walls would have not fallen.

No matter what our circumstances appear to be, if we want to see the victory manifest in our lives, we have to shout the victory! When we shout our praises to God, walls—of doubt, lack, sickness, oppression, and unforgiveness—collapse. When we hit an obstacle that is keeping us from possessing what God has promised us, it is time to shout bondages, strongholds, and hindrances out of our lives in the name of Jesus. Shout doubt and fear out!

God has the power to do more than we could ever ask or think. God has the ability to do as He chooses. And when we are in obedient faith, God will take care of the walls in our lives!

Hebrews 11:30 tells us that by faith, the walls of Jericho fell after the people had marched around them for seven days. This is what biblical faith and confidence look like. Joshua and the people of God demonstrated confidence in the power of God, and they marched until the walls fell!

Maybe you should ask yourself today, *Do I have that kind of confidence?* Philippians 1:6 (NASB) says, "For I am confident of this very thing, that He who began a good work among you will complete it by the day of Christ Jesus." You and I can be confident in the finished work of Christ! Whatever He starts, He will finish. Whatever He promised, He will accomplish. He will do His will in your life.

So, when you shout unto God with passion, God will release His power, and walls will fall. Proclaim this today: "God is my confidence. My confidence is not in my own ability. I will not put my faith in my own ability to accomplish the work in my life, but I will put my faith in God's ability. And I believe that every wall, every barrier, every obstacle is coming down by the power of your Holy Spirit. I will not allow unforgiveness, fears, insecurities, and inadequacies to become a snare that will keep me from accessing everything God has for me. I won't give up. I will not back down. I will stay in faith, and I will trust God for the outcome. I stake my claim. I stand my ground, and I will shout for joy 'til the walls come down!"

Scan to download the song from this chapter.

PRAYER

God, my confidence is not in me. I will not put my faith in my own ability—instead, I will put my faith in Yours. Every wall, every barrier, every obstacle is coming down by the power of your Holy Spirit. I will not allow my fears and insecurities to become snares that keep me from accessing everything You have for me. I won't give up! I won't back down. I will stay in faith and trust You for the outcome! Today, I stake my claim, I stand my ground, and I will shout for joy—'til the walls come down! In Jesus's name. Amen.

THREE

I'M GONNA WIN

I'm gonna win
I'm gonna win
I'm gonna win
'Cause God says so

I am clothed in peace
I am royalty
I have been redeemed
'Cause God says so
I have all I need
I have authority
I can do all things
Nothing is impossible

The name of Jesus is glorious
The name of Jesus is glorious
The name of Jesus is glorious
There's power in the name

Jesus
Jesus
Jesus

There's power in that name
I was created to make
    Your praise glorious
I was created to make
    Your praise glorious

Your name is power
You're my strong tower
That's why we sing

I'm gonna win
I'm gonna win
I'm gonna win
'Cause God says so

MUSIC AND LYRICS BY MARTHA MUNIZZI, DAVID OUTING, SHARON ANN

23

T he year 2020 was crazy for all of us. No one could have foreseen a worldwide pandemic, much less a massive shutdown of life as we knew it. At first, we thought the quarantine wouldn't last long, but then, it was clear that it was going to change our lives completely, and it did. We didn't know what the coming weeks and months were going to look like, so we just settled in and hoped for the best.

In 2015, my husband, Dan, and I, along with our three adult children—Danielle, Nicole, and Nathan—planted EpicLife Church in Orlando, Florida. We knew pastoring would require a lot of sacrifice, but we believed God had spoken to us to limit travel and start a church. Planting a church is hard enough; leading people through a pandemic was a huge challenge. We shut down our Sunday services for a few weeks and, like most churches, moved our church online. By April, we realized that we weren't going to be celebrating Easter with two services, Easter egg hunts, and a big celebration as we'd planned.

We started to realize that, based on what the media was telling us, 2020 was not going to be a normal year. We would need to find a way to get through it and just survive.

Once we reopened, we only gathered at 50-percent capacity because of social distancing guidelines. Since our five-year anniversary was coming up, we wanted to celebrate with our church family. However, we opted to keep the celebration small. We decided we would keep the plans simple—but still special—since five years is a benchmark year for a church.

Our team came up with the idea to write a song to commemorate the occasion. We reached out to David Outing, an incredibly talented producer who is also a friend of ours, to see if he would work with us, and within a couple of days, we had our first writing session. My daughters, Nicole and Danielle, and I met in our recording studio.

When we had written four songs in just a few hours, we knew that we were supposed to do something bigger than just produce one song for our church. God wanted to do something in the fourth quarter of 2020 that would redeem the entire year! His plans are so much bigger than ours!

We started writing in mid-October, and before we had even finished writing all of the songs we would need for an entire album, we scheduled and started planning and promoting a live recording for November 20, 2020. That's often called "Putting the cart before the horse." In less than thirty days, we wrote, produced, and recorded a live album at our home church. So much for keeping it simple!

Because 2020 was full of setbacks, disappointments, and tremendous loss for so many people all over the world, I wanted to write something that would remind all of us that God is still in control, and pandemic or no pandemic, we were still going to come out of 2020 victorious. We *would* win! David, our producer, and I wanted to capture the musicality, the joy, and the celebration of "Glorious," one of the songs that I am most known for, and write an updated version with a similar sound but a new declaration.

One day, while in the grocery store, I got the idea for "Glorious 2.0." Right there in the grocery store, in the middle of the frozen food section, the song came flowing out! "I'm gonna win. I'm gonna win. I'm gonna win cuz God says so!" I recorded it on my phone as quickly as I could and sent it to my producer. It's funny because there have been plenty of times when I've had an idea or written a song in an unusual moment or location but never in the frozen food section!

As I finished writing the song, I asked myself, *What does it mean to win?* Sometimes winning can look very different than what you expect. Many people think winning is based on numbers, statistics, big crowds, or lots of money. The truth is that winning is an attitude. It's a mindset and a posture. It's a position of faith, knowing that because of the finished work of Jesus on the cross, we've already won every battle. So now we learn how to overcome in our day-to-day lives. In other words, we fight to win from a place OF victory, not FOR victory.

> *Many people think winning is based on numbers, statistics, big crowds, or lots of money. The truth is that winning is an attitude. It's a mindset and a posture. It's a position of faith, knowing that because of the finished work of Jesus on the cross, we've already won every battle.*

I know what it feels like to actually be the underdog. An underdog is someone no one expects to win. Have you ever felt like you were the underdog? What does winning look like from an underdog's position? Sometimes, the process of winning won't look like success at all.

A few years ago, I was invited to sing at one of the largest conferences in the nation. There were many well-known ministers, leaders, preachers, pastors, and songwriters from all over the world coming to minister as well, so it was a huge honor. Many of the speakers were scheduled to officiate a breakout session in one of the large conference rooms during the event. Since the conference had over thirty thousand people in attendance, the breakout sessions were quite large as well, and each of the conference rooms sat between 1,000 and 2,000 people.

Many of the speakers and musical guests had merchandise tables set up in the lobby, and my product table was adjacent to a well-known pastor. I watched as hundreds of people surrounded his table, clamoring for his books and ministry material, while every other table had no customers at all. That was humbling! It does not feel like winning when your merchandise isn't selling, and the person at the table right next to yours is selling out! *Or it did not feel like I was winning when my CDs weren't selling, and the person at the table right next to me was selling out while I watched!*

I had to pray and ask the Holy Spirit to keep my heart right during that experience.

Directly behind our merchandise tables were the entrances to the breakout sessions. The room my pastor friend was scheduled to speak in was right next to the famous minister's room. Although I was honored to sing and lead worship and excited for my friend, my excitement turned to disappointment as I stood and watched people pour into the famous speaker's session and trickle into ours. At least one thousand people had filled the famous minister's room, and it was becoming clear that our session would only have two hundred or fewer attendees.

Both sessions started at the same time, and the noises already coming through the walls of the packed room were getting louder. I walked into my session, saw fewer people in the room, and felt so bad for my friend. This had to hurt! I quickly notified my face to shake off the look of frustration and get ready to lead the handful of people into God's presence. The noises of shouting, chanting, clapping, and dancing were so loud in the adjacent room that we could hardly hear ourselves talk. I stepped on the stage next to my friend, and as I scanned the very small crowd, I started to notice the people who came to hear my friend speak. He was and is a seasoned pastor, and many pastors and leaders from all over the world call him their pastor. He is a leader of leaders and a pastor of pastors. Everyone in the room pastored churches of hundreds as well as thousands of people, and they had all come to hear him speak. They could have followed the crowd next door because that's where all the excitement was.

I leaned over to my friend and said, "I know the room next door is packed with people, but THIS room is filled with people who MAKE an impact! You are potentially speaking to hundreds of thousands of people by speaking to the pastors and leaders in this room!" My friend wasn't as concerned about the numbers as I was, but he's still human. He whispered into my ear, "Thank you! I needed to hear that."

The powerful message he preached to that small crowd, I believe, impacted far more than the people in the room. And, interestingly enough, years later, the famous speaker with the large crowd was caught in a scandal that destroyed his family, his ministry, and his legacy

Be careful not to follow the crowd. A big crowd doesn't necessarily mean you're winning. Sometimes it's in the smallest moment that God is doing the most! What He's doing in you is far greater than what He's doing for you or even through you. Do you see how important the right perspective is to winning? Had my friend been insecure and petty, he could have refused to speak in his session because the noise was so loud coming from the other room. Had he done that, he would have disappointed a lot of people who follow and respect him. He set a great example for all us because he didn't allow the pressure to discourage him. He didn't see himself as a loser. He wasn't the underdog. He didn't consider himself that at all. He did what God had sent him there to do, regardless of the outcome. That's how you win. Ask the Holy Spirit to help you learn how to shift your perspective and attitude in difficult or disappointing situations, so you start to see things the way God does.

Don't waste time feeling sorry for yourself if you think you're losing. Losing is sometimes a big part of winning. You can learn so much by losing. I know that doesn't make you feel any better, but it's true. Losing is a part of life. Not everybody wins. There are always losers. Celebrities and musicians get nominated for Golden Globes, Oscars, and Grammys, but the majority go home disappointed. When one team wins the Super Bowl, thirty-one others are defeated, but those who have what it takes will emerge from the loss stronger than before.

I love this quote from Hall of Fame basketball coach Morgan Wootten: "You learn more from losing than winning. You learn how to keep going."

Keep going! You are going to win! In fact, if you are still moving forward, you are already winning! How do I know? God says so!

Take time to read this scripture today and commit it to memory. Second Corinthians 2:14 (NKJV) says, "But thanks be to God, who always leads us in triumph in Christ." God says "always," so He means ALWAYS! How do I know I'm gonna win? God says so!

Speak this declaration today:

I will keep moving forward.

I won't give up.

God is able to do more than I could ever imagine in my life.

Today, I give God praise for giving me the victory in every situation, no matter what it looks like.

 Scan to download the song from this chapter.

I will put my trust in God, and I will win!!

PRAYER

Father, I thank You because I know all power belongs to You! Teach my hand to war and my tongue to battle. You are my King, my fortress, my strength, and my redeemer. Today, I ask You to fill me with a spirit of wisdom, understanding, and knowledge that creates success and victory. Fill me with a spirit of excellence that makes for success, and give me grace for stick-ability, boldness, and tenacity to stay the course and hold on to victory. I am who You say I am. In Jesus's name. Amen!

FOUR

WORTHY

♪

Everything You created
With one word
Everything came into existence
Heaven and Earth
You spoke life into me
You breathed life into
   these bones
You spoke life into me

Jesus You are
Worthy of all the glory
Worthy of all the praise
Worthy of all the glory
Thank You, Lord, for
   everything

For all that You have done
For all that is to come
Thank You, Lord

MUSIC AND LYRICS BY MARTHA MUNIZZI, DANIELLE MUNIZZI, DAVID OUTING

*In every situation [no matter what the circumstances]
be thankful and continually give thanks to God; for
this is the will of God for you in Christ Jesus.*
—1 THESSALONIANS 5:18 (AMP)

I love every word that has been given to us in Scripture; however, if there was only one verse that teaches us how to live a victorious life, this one would be it. This scripture gives us specific instruction and confidence to live in God's will. Have you ever asked the age-old question, "What is God's will for my life?" This is the answer! God's will for you is that you would be thankful! (1 Thessalonians 5:18)

 Is it possible to be thankful in every situation? It is not an easy task, but it is entirely possible.

I know what you're probably thinking: *It's not that easy. How can I be thankful when my life is so difficult? How can I be thankful when my heart has been broken by someone I loved?*

Is it possible to be thankful in every situation? It is not an easy task, but it is entirely possible.

The personal story I have saved for this last chapter is one I don't share often. It's not that I have any issues with telling this story, it's just that God has healed me completely from the memories and trauma I experienced as a child. When I was fourteen years old, I told my mother that a family member had been molesting me, my sisters, and my cousins for several years. It started when we were all very young and continued until we were teenagers. My mother was horrified and in shock. She didn't know what to say and certainly didn't know what to do. This was not a topic that was regularly discussed in our culture at that time. This was not a topic discussed in the mainstream media, either, so she was totally unprepared as to how to handle it. I begged her to keep it a secret because I was so afraid of what would happen if anyone else found out.

She comforted me as best she could, although her heart was crushed by my dark secret. The next day, I came home from school, walked into our house and saw my Dad sitting in his chair sobbing.

I knew instantly my mother had shared the terrible news with my father. He was devastated that this family member would commit such an indefensible violation against his daughters and nieces. Later that day, my father confronted the family member, and all hell broke loose.

The family member denied it, my grandmother accused us of causing it, and from that moment on, my life as I knew it changed forever. This dark secret was so destructive that it wasn't long before most of my family members and their marriages were destroyed. My father left my mother two years later, and for the first time, I knew what betrayal felt like. My father said he believed our story but left us to move in with his parents. My mother faced life as a single mom with no real skills or education beyond her high school diploma. My father served my mother with divorce papers, but she refused to sign them. She believed for almost a year after my father left that God would restore their marriage. My sisters and I wanted to believe with her for reconciliation, but we knew the sad truth. My father wanted to move on with his life, and he had no intention of including any of us in it.

One day, I came home from work, and my mother was in the fetal position on the floor, crying out to God. She had been trying to hold back her emotions and stay strong, but she finally broke under the pressure. I walked into the house and saw her lying on the floor. I rushed to her side, knelt down, and whispered in her ear, "Mom, you have to let Dad go. It's been a year. It's time to move on and trust God to restore in the way He chooses! Please just sign the divorce papers, and let Dad go!"

As she wept and wept, I did the only thing I could do, and that was pray. It wasn't long until I felt the presence of the Holy Spirit come into the room. God began to speak through me, and I started prophesying over my mother. I started rebuking the devil off of her life and told doubt and fear to leave her. I declared that God was going to restore her the way He restored Job and that, although she lost someone she loved, God was going give her a thousand times more! I knew God was going to redeem my mother's life and that He would take care of our family. It didn't take long for our tears of grief to turn into thanksgiving. We got up from the floor thanking God that, in the middle of lack and uncertainty, a miracle was going to happen!

Several days later, my mother went to lunch with her pastor's wife and she told my mother she believed that she and my father would get back together. My mother drove home from that lunch very hopeful and excited, thinking that her miracle was on the way. Unfortunately, not only did we *not* get a miracle, as I mentioned in a previous chapter that six days after my mother signed the divorce papers, my father remarried. We were shocked. My sisters and I were so afraid to tell our mother the news. How would she react? Would the realization that she and our father would never reconcile break her? Would she scream and cry or become despondent?

We sat her down and, in very calm voices, we said, "Mom, we have some bad news. Please don't get upset. It's going to be okay." At first, she did what any other brokenhearted woman would do: she cried. For a few moments, she let out all the emotions she had been holding back. We sat and cried with her. But then, the most unusual thing happened. My mother stopped crying and started thanking God that at least her turmoil was over, and she could close that chapter of her life. It wasn't long into the prayer that she started giggling when she thought about how much time she'd spent believing Dad would come back. Within a few minutes, she was laughing out loud! Seeing her laugh made us laugh too. We had all cried so much over the previous two years that we decided we might as well laugh.

The more we laughed, the funnier it became. The irony that my mom had spent an entire year hoping to reconcile with my father, while the entire time he was already in another relationship, was actually hilarious in that moment. Have you ever laughed so hard you couldn't breathe? That was us! We were laughing so hard we had tears running down our faces. I can't explain it except it had to be the work of the Holy Spirit.

Only a few days earlier, she had been broken and hurting, feeling the hopelessness of her situation. Now, she was fulfilling the promise from God in Job 8:21(NIV) that says, "He will yet fill your mouth with laughter." The miracle we needed didn't come in the form we thought it would, but the reality that we could laugh over something so painful was all the miracle we needed.

> *The miracle we needed didn't come in the form we thought it would, but the reality that we could laugh over something so painful was all the miracle we needed.*

Proverbs 31:25 (NLT) says, "She is clothed with strength and dignity, and she laughs without fear of the future." None of us had any idea how great the future was about to become. It wasn't long before God brought an amazing man into my mother's life who swept her off of her feet. They fell in love, got married, and had twenty-five wonderful years together. God did exceedingly, abundantly, far above what we were asking Him to do. What started out as a tragedy—a family devastated by child abuse, divorce, and broken dreams—became a real-life Cinderella story.

Thanksgiving will provoke God's blessings to move in your favor—in your direction—and bring the deliverance you need. Being thankful in everything releases His joy which becomes your strength.

Is there a situation you're facing right now that is causing you anxiety and pressure, that's robbing you of joy? Is the shame of disappointment and heavy pressure causing anxiety and fear? It's time to find something to be thankful for! Did you know that pressure can sometimes end up being a privilege? When you're under pressure, you find out how strong you are. You discover how resilient you are. You realize God is your source, and He will never let you fall. Pressure will show you all the good things God has for you that are under the surface. All good things in life are *never* found on the surface. Think about it: precious minerals are extracted only after pressure has been applied. Diamonds and other precious jewels and minerals have to be mined and excavated. Pressure has to be applied for them to come to the surface.

Pressure is a privilege! If you're under pressure right now, it just means good things are about to show up! Power is released in thanksgiving. In John 11:41, Jesus gave thanks, and Lazarus was raised from the dead! God will resurrect your dead dreams and release favor and blessing in your life if you make the decision to give Him thanks—even for the struggle. Unfortunately, you may not be able to control the specific outcomes, but you can give God thanks in everything.

Scan to download the song from this chapter.

PRAYER

God, I will be thankful today in everything! I know there is power in thanksgiving to release the breakthrough I need. Today, I will praise You—You are good, and You are worthy. You have always been faithful to me, and You will never leave me or forsake me. I am so thankful I can laugh without any fear of the future. Thank You for the struggle and the pressure because I know Your hand of favor is on me, and good things are coming to the surface of my life. I will be thankful in everything because this is Your will for me. I love You, Jesus, with all that I am. Amen.

FIVE

NEW SEASON

♪

It's a new season
It's a new day
Fresh anointing
Is flowing my way
It's a season of power
And prosperity
It's a new season
Coming to me

The devil's time is up—no
longer can he bother me
'Cause the Creator of the
universe
He fathers me
And it's transferable your
children's children
will be free
It's a new season

If you don't know by now, you
need to know it's Jubilee

Where debts are canceled and
your children walk in victory
It's all available to you right
now just taste and see
It's a new season

The new millennium presents
a new horizon and
No greater time for us to make
a choice and take a stand
All that we need is resting
safely in the Master's hand
It's a new season

All that was stolen is returned
to you a hundred fold
Tried in the fire but you're
coming out gold
Cling to His hand, yes, to
every promise take a hold
It's a new season

It's a new season
It's a new day
Fresh anointing
Is flowing my way

It's a season of power
and prosperity
It's a new season coming to me

MUSIC AND LYRICS BY DERICK THOMAS & ISRAEL HOUGHTON

I f you've ever binge-watched your favorite TV show, you know what it feels like to anxiously anticipate the date when the new season comes out. With every new season, exciting plotlines unfold, additional characters are revealed, and nail-biting cliffhangers are resolved.

New seasons in our lives are exciting because they represent the beginning of a new experience. You're starting over but at a different level. Every new season requires the same focus that the previous one required. The same principles or steps apply, but you learned a lot from the last season, and now you can put your experiences to work as you walk through the new season.

My husband, Dan, and I have been married for thirty-five years, so to say we've been through a lot of seasons together would be an understatement. We met when we were very young. We were introduced by a mutual friend of ours who was putting together a worship band. This person was looking for musicians and singers to travel to local churches and ministries to lead worship. He also recruited my sisters, Marvelyne and Mary. We were the worship leaders, and Dan and his brother played bass and drums in the band. This was my dream! I was only sixteen years old, and the biggest thing I had been a part of up until that time was serving in almost every capacity in my Mom and Dad's church in Orlando.

The worship band didn't last that long, but it was the catalyst God used to bring Dan and me together. We fell in love pretty quickly, dated for three years, and married in 1987. Dan is a phenomenal musician and producer as well as extremely gifted administratively. For the first fifteen years of our marriage, Dan was a home builder for several large companies in Central Florida. I worked off and on at small jobs to make ends meet, and after five years, we welcomed Danielle, our first baby, into the family. Two and one-half years later, Nicole was born, and two years after that, we had Nathan.

Every new baby birthed a new season of blessing in our lives, but it also brought challenges. I stopped working full-time when Danielle was born, so Dan's paycheck had to make ends meet. That was a very difficult season financially for us. We learned to trust God in ways we never had before. We struggled to pay our bills on one income with three kids, and we were so strapped we were using credit cards to pay for our groceries. It wasn't long before we were in debt—$40k of debt! For a young family, that was an overwhelming reality. We had no idea how we were going to pay it. It was going to take years to pay off that much debt! All of our income was going out to pay for food, diapers, and monthly bills so we had no savings and no emergency fund.

One day I called my mother and shared all of my frustrations with her. She listened patiently to all of my complaints about our financial situation and how hard things were for us. After listening intently, she gave me these brilliant words of wisdom, "Martha, I don't know what else to tell you except this . . . you're gonna have to learn to turn your bad days into good days and just trust the Lord until this season changes!"

Those words were not what I wanted to hear but I knew I needed to hear them. She was so right! I had to learn to find the good things in a bad season because that's what grownups do! Mature believers who trust God know how to create joy when life is hard. They master the skill of holding on to their joy and peace during a difficult season because they know God will see them through.

After hearing my mother's sage advice, I decided to change my attitude and to start looking at my situation from a new perspective. I realized that I was making a bad season worse by focusing on what I didn't have, instead of focusing on what I did have. I started applying my mother's advice immediately and I'm so glad I did! I was able to find lots of ways to enjoy time and have fun with my young family that didn't cost a lot of money. Looking back now, I actually miss that season of our lives. Our kids didn't miss out on anything, and they had no idea we were struggling financially.

Somehow, in our lack, God provided for all of our needs! If you're in a hard season right now learn how to turn your bad days into good days. Don't miss out on the blessing of the season you're in. It's just a season and there's a better one coming! I had no way of knowing that new seasons of blessing, open doors, creative ideas, and resources were being prepared for us. We had no idea the breakthrough that was ahead for us and could have never seen what God was about to do in our lives.

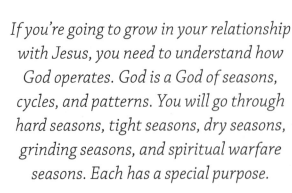

If you're going to grow in your relationship with Jesus, you need to understand how God operates. God is a God of seasons, cycles, and patterns. You will go through hard seasons, tight seasons, dry seasons, grinding seasons, and spiritual warfare seasons. Each has a special purpose.

God established specific principles regarding times and seasons in His word. Solomon described God's plan in Ecclesiastes 3:1 (NASB,

1995): "There is an appointed time for everything. And there is a time for every event under heaven. . . ." There is a

Scan to download the song from this chapter.

time for everything! A time to laugh, cry, mourn, dance, everything! There are natural seasons, cycles, and patterns, and there are spiritual seasons as well. If you're going to grow in your relationship with Jesus, you need to understand how God operates. God is a God of seasons, cycles, and patterns. You will go through hard seasons, tight seasons, dry seasons, grinding seasons, and spiritual warfare seasons. Each has a special purpose.

Some prepare us by allowing God to make much-needed changes in us. Some are a time for strengthening and maturing. When God wants you to examine your heart and motives, He will sometimes take you through a season of isolation or a winter season. Seasons of pruning are difficult but so vital to our spiritual health. God will prune us to shape and mold us. As hard as some seasons can be, there are spring seasons that represent growth, joy, flourishing, new life, opportunities, and breakthroughs! No matter how hard a season may be, you're growing, changing, and getting stronger. You're putting seed in the ground. Your roots are growing deeper, and a harvest is coming—greater anointing is coming to you. God has promised to bless you if you won't quit or give up! Be encouraged that just like the natural seasons change, so will the season you are currently in change.

There is a new season coming if you will just hold on! Everything you're going through is preparing you for the greater blessing God is preparing FOR you and preparing you FOR! Don't get depressed—get happy! Get your hopes up, and remind yourself that seasons change. Yours will too!

PRAYER

Thank You for Your faithfulness in guiding me through the new things You are doing in my life. I am so grateful for every opportunity You bring and every open door You have laid out before me. Help me to be faithful in each and every opportunity You bring to me. Thank You for everything and everyone You have pruned out of my life, so I can flourish in my new season. Help me trust You as I walk through new doors and new opportunities. Give me the wisdom to see what You are doing even in the dark seasons of my life. I declare this is my season of favor, abundance and open doors—and I will hold on to Your promises as I enter into the new day You are laying out before me! In Jesus's name. Amen.

SIX

GRATEFUL

♪

When I think of the
   things You've done
The life You gave
And the war You've won
I can't help but remember love
And I'm so grateful

What can I say
But, "Thank You, Jesus"?
And what can I do
But give You praise?
You are good
And I'm so grateful
Your love endures forever
I love You, Lord

The sin that stained
And the shame I carried
Washed away where
The Son was buried
But thank You, Jesus
You rose again
And I'm so grateful, grateful

I'll sing it again
And again and again
Forever and ever
I'll sing it
I love You, Lord

MUSIC AND LYRICS BY DANIELLE MUNIZZI & DAVID OUTING

*Give thanks in all circumstances; for this is
God's will for you in Christ Jesus.*
—1 THESSALONIANS 5:18 (NIV)

A fter eight years of serving in our local church at the time, in 2001 we launched out on our own into an unknown world, having no idea what was ahead of us. Of course, we had big dreams, but we had absolutely no way to accomplish any of those dreams on our own. Not only that, we were still in debt with nothing substantial to show for it. As a young couple, we were living in real time—what Robert Kiyosaki writes about in his book *Rich Dad, Poor Dad*.[1] We had gone from two people and two incomes to a one-income household trying to raise three small children. It wasn't like we bought a big house, car, or expensive things; we were just trying to survive.

Dan and I were overwhelmed with the debt we were facing, and it looked like it would be years before we were financially stable. I remember crying out to God asking Him for a financial break-through because it felt as if we were in a chokehold, and there was no way out. What do you do when you know God has great things for you, but lack, sickness, or some other difficulty has you trapped? I knew what it felt like to really believe that God was going to do something great in the future; I just had to get through my present situation.

I would love to be able to say that my difficult season only lasted a few weeks. Unfortunately, that's not the case. God was teaching us how to trust Him, so He allowed the season to last longer than we had hoped it would. As I mentioned earlier, for the first fifteen years of our marriage, my husband Dan built homes for several large home builders in Central Florida. He became one of the top superintendents of a major home-building company. He was doing very well at the beginning of our marriage, but once kids started coming, our financial

---

1 Robert T. Kiyosaki, *Rich Dad Poor Dad: With Updates for Today's World and 9 New Study Session Sections* (Scottsdale, AZ: Plata Publishing, 2017).

challenges began. We had to learn to trust God when it looked like there was no way out.

I remember one time in our lives when we really struggled to make ends meet, and Dan considered getting a second job delivering pizzas. I was actually excited about the idea because . . . free pizza! I look back at that season, and although I would never want to repeat it, I'm so grateful for it. It taught us to stay close to God and that He is our source. Your job is not your source—God is your source. And free pizza is a blessing when you're broke!

Not only did we walk away from working full-time for our church, but we walked away from our friends, family, and what we thought was our future. We were young, and there was so much we didn't understand at the time. As time passed, we began to realize we had put too much faith in people to tell us what to do, and God was teaching us to hear and follow His voice. I'm grateful for the men and women in my life who have mentored, challenged, and shaped me into who I am. But I learned a long time ago not to put my trust in people. Love them, honor them, and respect them—but they are not your source.

You may have had your hopes dashed or your expectations unmet by someone you served and put your trust in. What if that job ended because God had more for you, and you wouldn't have left any other way? What if the promise that was made to you wasn't God's plan? Maybe the reason you didn't get promoted is because God had something even better in mind. What if the relationship ended because it wasn't God's best for you?

When a mother eagle builds a nest, she first weaves together thorny branches. Then, she lays soft filler on top. As the baby eaglets grow, the space gets smaller. In their reluctance to leave, the mother eagle begins to remove the soft filler. The eaglets cry since thorns poke and prod them as they try to get comfortable in the nest.

I believe that God will put thorns in your nest when He's ready for you to fly. Don't misunderstand and think the thorns are there to destroy you. The thorns are there to poke, prod, and aggravate you just enough to get your attention. Why? Because it's time to fly! It's time to take your next step and do what God is calling you to do. Let those thorny people and situations go; forgive as quickly as possible. Don't spend time crying over disappointment or rejection. Don't ever allow unforgiveness or bitterness from something someone said or didn't say to stay lodged in your heart and keep you from the greater things God has for you. Stay grateful! In everything—Give Thanks!

Don't spend time crying over disappointment or rejection. Don't ever allow unforgiveness or bitterness from something someone said or didn't say to stay lodged in your heart and keep you from the greater things God has for you. Stay grateful! In everything—Give Thanks!

God is doing something that you can't see, and if you are holding onto offense, you will miss out on what God is doing. Focusing on your hurt will distract you from focusing on your future. Whenever feelings of insecurity from rejection overtake you, practice gratitude right then. Don't wait for the negative feelings to pass on their own. Negative feelings will fade when you reframe your thoughts on the promises of God.

Stay grateful to God for everything! First Thessalonians 5:18 (NASB, 1995) says, "In *everything* give thanks; for *this* is God's will for your life" (emphasis added). That's what the struggle is all about. Learn through every difficult trial to put your trust in Jesus!

The title of this chapter is "Grateful." Take time to listen to this song today! Start singing: *What can I say but, "Thank You, Jesus?" What can I do but give You praise? You are good, and I'm so grateful. Your love endures forever!* He's good, and I'm grateful. That's it! That's God's will for your life.

The rest of this song is simple, but it will change your mindset if you will sing it: *I'll sing it again and again and again. Forever and ever, I'll sing it again!*

Can you imagine how much happier we would be if we decided to just be grateful and give thanks in everything? Not some things. Not a lot of things. Not when everything is going our way, and our bills are paid—but in everything! That means, when I'm sick, broke, or disappointed, I'm grateful. When I didn't get what I wanted, I'm still grateful!

When my kids were little, and I took them to a store, I would allow each one of them to buy a small toy. I didn't have to do that. They had a lot of toys, but I just wanted to make them happy. Nothing would frustrate me more than when, after I bought them what they wanted, they cried for more. The worst moment was when one of them got so mad at me for not buying them a second toy that they threw the first one out of the cart and onto the floor. I put both toys back and didn't get them anything. I had no problem with leaving the store empty-handed. I taught my kids early on that if they

Scan to download the song from this chapter.

want Momma to bless them with more, they had better be grateful for what they have. God requires the very same thing.

If you want God to do more in your life . . . be grateful!

If you want God's will for your life . . . be grateful!

If you want more peace . . . be grateful!

If you want more joy . . . be grateful!

If you want more of Jesus . . . be grateful!

The discipline of being grateful in everything is not easy, but that's where you will see the biggest growth and the greatest blessings!

PRAYER

Thank You, Lord, for the blessings You have bestowed on my life. You have provided me with more than I ever could have imagined. You have surrounded me with people who always look out for me. You have given me family and friends who bless me every day with kind words and actions.

I am so grateful for Your peace in my mind, Your joy in my heart, and Your presence in my life. Help me to be disciplined in showing gratitude more and more every day. Thank You for the spiritual growth and maturity taking place in my life as I am becoming more grateful for all You have done! In Jesus's name. Amen.

SEVEN

HOLY SPIRIT, FILL THIS ROOM

Holy Spirit, fill this room *Shekinah glory, sweet perfume* *We need Your presence—* *we need You* *Holy Spirit, fill this room*	*Holy Spirit, fill this room* *Shekinah glory, sweet perfume* *We need Your presence—* *we need You* *Holy Spirit, fill this room*

MUSIC AND LYRICS BY MARTHA MUNIZZI

"Holy Spirit, Fill this Room" is one of the first songs I ever wrote. At the time, I needed direction and clarity about what God was calling me to do. I knew something big was in my future, but I had no idea how to take the first step.

Its words were written out of a desire to go deeper into God's presence and hear God's voice on a deeper level. "Shekinah glory" was a risk to put in the lyrics of a song, but I settled on keeping it once I began to research its meaning. Although the word *shekinah* does not actually appear in the Bible, in Hebrew, it can mean "He caused to dwell," and it was the term given to a divine visitation of *Yahweh*. Shekinah glory is the pillar of cloud by day and the pillar of fire by night that guided the Israelites through the desert after their exodus from Egypt:

And they moved on from Succoth and encamped at Etham, on the edge of the wilderness. And the Lord went before them by day in a pillar of cloud to lead them along the way, and by night in a pillar of fire to give them light, that they might travel by day and by night. The pillar of cloud by day and the pillar of fire by night did not depart from before the people. —Exodus 13:20-22 (ESV)

God's presence went before them and led them day and night. It never left them.

Jesus gave us the promise of the Holy Spirit. Now, instead of being led by pillars of cloud and fire, we rely on the inner voice and the promptings of the Holy Spirit Himself.

To hear the voice of God more clearly, I needed the Holy Spirit to teach me how to trust in what I couldn't see in my natural ability. Although I had big dreams and desires, my mind could have never conceived what God was preparing for me.

First Corinthians 2:9-11 (NIV) says:

What no eye has seen, what no ear has heard, and what no human mind has conceived—the things God has prepared for those who love him—these are the things God has revealed to us by his Spirit. The Spirit searches all things, even the deep things of God. For who knows a person's thoughts except their own Spirit within them? In the same way no one knows the thoughts of God except the Spirit of God.

To fully understand the Holy Spirit, you must first understand who He is not. He is not a power or a force or energy. The Holy Spirit is a person. He is not an it—He is a He. As a believer, you have the Spirit of God living inside of you. If you don't understand who He is, you won't relate to Him as a person. If you believe that the Holy Spirit is an energy force, then you will relate to Him as energy—not as a person. You won't understand Him, so you will keep Him at arms-length. Acts 1:8 (NKJV) says, "You shall *receive* power" (emphasis added). The Holy Ghost is not power. He enables you to receive power, but He is more than power.

The Holy Spirit is a person. He is the Spirit of God. He has a personality. It's so important to know this because if you don't understand who He is, then you will override His advice and take your own. You won't recognize His worth, and you won't respect His role in your life. You will begin to think that you are smarter than the Holy Spirit. Then, when you are disappointed with the outcome of your decisions, you will wonder what happened. Sometimes, we even blame God for our mess when He didn't have anything to do with it!

The Holy Spirit can be trusted because He knows what you don't know. He's intelligent. First Corinthians 2:10 (KJV) says, "But God hath revealed them unto us by His Spirit. For the Spirit searcheth all things, yea, the deep things of God." The Holy Spirit has an intelligence that searches even the deepest of things. What are the deep things? He knows what is in the mind and the heart of God, the divine counsel, and things far beyond human understanding. He knows the secret hidden things. God is omniscient—all-knowing. He knows the end from the beginning.

> *Sometimes we make decisions based on the past and the present, but the Holy Spirit makes decisions knowing the past, the present, and the future. . . . He knows exactly where you came from, what your background is, and what is needed in order to bring you out, so you cannot ignore Him.*

Sometimes we make decisions based on the past and the present, but the Holy Spirit makes decisions knowing the past, the present, and the future. The Holy Spirit already knows how things are going to turn out. He knows whether this is going to work for you twenty years from now. He knows exactly where you came from, what your background is, and what is needed in order to bring you out, so you cannot ignore Him. You make a decision every day whether you will accept His wisdom over your own.

Why is it important to hear the voice of the Holy Spirit? Because your wisdom is not enough. You can't get it right on your own. You don't have the ability to understand the mysteries of God's will and all that He has for you. There are mysteries that God will help you discover. He wants to show you where the keys are to unlock the destiny He has for you. You can't do that by yourself. You need Him!

Zechariah 4:6 (NIV) says, "'Not by might nor by power, but by my Spirit,' says the LORD Almighty." This means that you need His Spirit to speak to you, so you need to learn how to hear His voice. Our lives are shaped by God's Word, but there are some things the Bible doesn't specify, so you need His Spirit to learn how to hear His voice.

Think about it for a minute. There are no scriptures telling you whom to marry, where to live, or what your talents are. You can study the Word until you turn blue in the face, but until you hear the Holy Spirit, you won't have clear direction as to the details of what God has designed for your life. My kids have asked me, "Mom, how do you know if that person is the one?" I tell them, "You absolutely know it! You know in your spirit that this is going to be the person that you're going to spend the rest of your life with. You just feel it. There's a connection, and you feel a confirmation in your spirit!"

AND . . . there's fruit that comes from the relationship. There's an anointing—a yes! And if you don't have that yes, then don't do it. It doesn't matter how cute or how fine they are or how much money they have. Don't do it. A person can be rich and crazy! A person can be cute and crazy. You want to connect with somebody through a revelation of the Spirit that you are meant to be together. This is important information that Scripture may not dictate to you. We need the Holy Spirit to get down into the details of what or who is right for us.

That's what the Holy Spirit is in your life to do. He'll lead you into all truth, so you won't be led into error. The enemy sends confusion so that you'll be in turmoil and so that you don't have clear direction. God is not the author of confusion. The Holy Spirit wants to show you paths and directions and give you wisdom you couldn't know in your own ability, so you won't be deceived by the world around you and waste your life on things that have no eternal value. The thief (the devil, Satan) comes only to steal, kill, and destroy. But Jesus came to give you life—and life MORE ABUNDANTLY!

The Holy Spirit takes you into the supernatural realm and brings your future before you. He gives you the ability to see what's in your future. He can reveal hidden things to you. *Merriam-Webster's Dictionary* says that to reveal means "to make known through divine inspiration; to make (something secret or hidden) publicly or generally known."[2] It means to unveil. The Holy Spirit unveils the hidden things, and He desires to show you the things that you can't see.

Let me ask you. How much time do you spend listening to the Holy Spirit? You may have been in church for years and never have been taught or never have learned how to listen to the voice of the Holy Spirit. There have been times during a worship service when the Holy

---

2 "Reveal," *Merriam-Webster Dictionary*, https://www.merriam-webster.com/dictionary/reveal.

Spirit will impress on me to sing a certain song. It may not be a song I was prepared to sing or had rehearsed, but in that moment, I know the Holy Spirit wants me to follow His prompting and not stick to my set list. For some reason, He wants that song sung in the service. When I change my plan and obey Him, the Holy Spirit takes over the room. I know I got it right by listening to the Holy Spirit because the shift in the room is evident. I've been in hundreds of worship services in my lifetime, so I have experienced this many times. To hear God's voice, you must eliminate all other voices and tune in to His.

One of the greatest enemies to really knowing and hearing the voice of the Holy Spirit is busyness. When your life is full of clutter and busyness and stress, it is hard to hear the Holy Spirit. It's hard to hear His voice in a storm. You need a calm place. You need to be still, according to Psalm 46:10 (NIV): "Be still and know that I am God." You'll never get a clear understanding of His voice in confusion. Just be still.

Another enemy of hearing God's voice is worry and anxiety. Philippians 4:6-7 (NIV) warns against this:

> *Do not be anxious about anything, but in everything by prayer and supplication with thanksgiving let your requests be made known to God. And the peace of God, which surpasses all understanding will guard your hearts and your minds in Christ Jesus.*

Max Lucado, a famous author, once said, "Anxiety is a meteor shower of what-ifs."[3]

What if my health begins to fail?

What if we can't save our marriage?

What if I can't pay my bills?

What if my friends reject me?

---

3 Max Lucado, "Anxiety Is Not Fun," *Max Lucado*, 17 Mar. 2020, https://maxlucado.com/listen/anxiety-is-not-fun/.

When you become over-whelmed with worry, anxiety, and fear, you could respond with panic, you might try to *Scan to download the song from this chapter.* control the situation, or you may react with aggression. Now, you're unable to hear the voice of the Holy Spirit. You're not listening to His voice because His voice is drowned out by fear.

Worship is the quickest way to tune into the Holy Spirit's voice because when you worship, He shows up. And when He shows up, His presence drives out fear! Refuse to be anxious. Pray with thanksgiving, and peace will guard your heart and your mind.

How did the psalmist David cope with anxiety? Psalm 16:2 (NIV) says: "Apart from you I have no good thing." David worshiped! Worship is intimacy with God. Intimacy is "in-to-me-see." When you worship, you tune in to God's voice, and you tune out the voice of anxiety. You shut out the voice of the enemy. Worship drives out fear and creates an atmosphere for the Holy Spirit to come and dwell and move and speak to you.

Let your prayer be, "Holy Spirit, I invite You into my life. Fill this room I'm in right now! Teach me how to hear Your voice more clearly. Change me. Holy Spirit, use me. I desire more of Your presence, Your power, and Your clear voice. I need Your presence every day. Fill me with all of You. In Jesus's name! Amen!"

PRAYER

Holy Spirit, I welcome You into my life to transform me and guide me in all I do. Show me how to live in the way that glorifies Jesus, and give me the wisdom I need. I welcome You into my home as I worship, read the Bible, and spend time in Your presence in fellowship with You. Help me to become more aware of Your presence and more sensitive to Your voice. Draw me closer to You, Holy Spirit. In Jesus's name I ask. Amen.

EIGHT

RENEW ME

♪

Renew me
Remake me
Create in me a clean
   heart, oh God
Restore me
Transform me
Create in me a clean
   heart, oh God
Change my heart, oh Lord
I'm broken before you now

Take me as I am
Receive this sacrifice

Don't cast me away from
   your presence
Renew a right spirit within me
'Cause my heart is
   broken before you
I bow down before
   you in worship

MUSIC AND LYRICS BY MARTHA MUNIZZI

O ne of the first big doors that opened for us when we first started traveling was an invitation to sing at a women's conference at a very large church in the U.S. The pastors were well-known, and they had invited a lot of famous people as guest speakers and singers to this conference. It was such a huge honor to be invited as a guest artist among so many important people!

To say I was excited would be an understatement. I had just recorded my first album, *Say the Name*, so I was thrilled to have the opportunity to minister at this conference and hoped I would sell a lot of CDs at my merch table.

I approached this experience with the mindset that this was a door that could easily lead to even more open doors for me. I had to do a good job. I had to be seen as more than a worship leader—I needed to be seen as a "gospel artist." I had spent many years serving in our local church, and now, it seemed that God was rewarding me for my faithfulness by allowing me to be on a bigger platform. I had a couple of friends who attended this church and worked on staff there as well, so I was really excited to see them and share this experience with them!

I arrived at the church early for my sound check and was greeted in the green room by one of these friends who was also the staff coordinator for all of the conference guests. It was her job to arrange the seating for the VIPs for the event. She was standing there with her headset on and her clipboard in hand, filled with the names of all the Very Important People that she was in charge of seating. After we hugged and got caught up, she took my husband Dan and me to the empty platform and said, "Once you finish your sound check, I'll show you where your seats for the conference will be. I have you seated on the platform in the VIP section!"

I couldn't get through soundcheck fast enough and find out where we would be sitting. All I could think about was the fact that I was finally going to be a "VIP!" All my years of serving were finally going to pay off. I was now going to be, a Very Important Person!

When it was time to be seated, my friend waved us over to the VIP section on the right side of the platform and began to look for our names on her clipboard. She smiled enthusiastically when she found our names and pointed to our seats. We were in the front row. *This is amazing!* I thought. *Tonight, I won't be seen as a choir member, a background singer, or the worship leader. Now I will be seen as a special guest soloist!*

The worship pastor of the church, who was also a good friend of ours, was standing next to the choir loft, watching us find our seats, and was happy to see us. His worship team and choir had been rehearsing my songs and would be singing with me during my set. I looked over at him as I very proudly sat in the VIP front row and nodded. He smiled back as if to say, "You made it, my friend!" As I settled into my seat, I took a moment to thank God for His incredible favor. I felt so honored and blessed to be seated among so many important leaders. I felt so humbled by it and knew I needed to take a minute and thank God for this opportunity. *God,* I prayed, *You are so good, and I am so humbled by this opportunity. . . .*

Suddenly, my thoughts were interrupted when my friend—the conference coordinator—tapped me on the shoulder, looked through the names on her clipboard, and sheepishly said to me, "I'm sorry. I put you in the wrong seats! If you don't mind, I need to move you over a few seats."

"No problem!" I responded. It was only a couple of seats over, and I was still in the front row.

A few minutes later, my friend with the clipboard came back over and again said to me, "I am so, so sorry, but we have a lot more VIPs coming than I thought. Do you mind moving back a row?"

My pride was a little hurt, but I obliged. I was still in the VIP section on the platform. I was just back a few more rows. I was frustrated, but I fixed my attitude, smiled, and moved to where I was told.

As the VIP section filled up, I couldn't stop smiling, seeing all of the celebrities who were being seated all around me. There were dignitaries, star athletes, and well-known personalities. And they were all about to hear me sing! Being surrounded by all of these notable people made a statement, and I could not believe that Dan and I would now be seen in front of everybody, surrounded by all of these VIPs! It was incredible, and I was a part of it!

As people began to pour into the church and the service was about to start, my "clipboard" friend came over to me one final time and said to me, "I am so, so sorry. I need more seats in this section for more VIPs. Do you mind moving just one more time?"

My heart sank. There were no more seats in the VIP section. It was completely full. Where was she going to put me?

She looked at me and said, "Would you mind if I sat you with the choir? I added a seat for you right next to our worship pastor."

I was about to be right back where I had started. I would no longer be seen among all the "important" people. I had been demoted to the level I thought I had just graduated from.

When I stood up and walked over to my new seat, I caught the eye of my other friend, the worship pastor, who was now welcoming me with open arms. He looked at me as if he knew I was disappointed, but he laughed and said, "Welcome back to the choir. We're happy to have you."

It's funny now, but it was crushing back then. One detail that can't be left out is that there was a half wall running across the stage, directly in front of the choir. This meant that when I sat down, only the top of my head could be seen! I sat in that chair thinking, God, are You kidding me? I was on my way to another level, and You put me back where I started? Now, no one will see me if I'm in the choir.

There's a wall in front of me, and I won't be recognized as a VIP. God, I'm grateful that I get to sing, but now everyone is going to think that I am part of the worship team instead of a guest artist.

As I held back tears, the Holy Spirit spoke to me: "Is this what it's about for you? Being seen? If being seen is so important to you, then there's a limit to how high I will take you."

Whoa! That snapped me out of it really quickly. I checked my heart, fixed my attitude, and got up and sang my songs with everything I had in me. After I finished singing, I walked back to my seat and disappeared into the choir stand.

> *Your heart is the center of your being, and from your heart, flow all of your feelings and thoughts. My heart was telling me something that wasn't true, my thoughts believed it, and my feelings responded to it. The only way for me to change my thoughts was to renew my mind and change my heart.*

Later in the service, the guest speaker was introduced by the host of the conference and I was excited to hear this very well-known female minister speak. As soon as she got to the podium, she took the mic and began to tell a story that immediately got my attention. She said that God had recently instructed her to gather her ministry team together every morning to pray at 6 am. During prayer one morning, someone on their team began to play a song they had never heard before. As they began singing the song, God's presence came in the room so strongly, that it tangibly shifted the atmosphere and they fell on their faces in worship.

She shared with the audience that night that for the last few weeks she had been singing this song all over the world in her meetings before she preached her message. That night she asked the musicians to follow her and began to sing the words that I knew very well because she was singing my song!

> *When we worship God and spend time in His word, the Holy Spirit illuminates what needs to be transformed and renewed in us, and has the power to change us.*

As I sat there with my head down, feeling rejected and unseen, this great woman of God started singing the words to my song "Say the Name." At first, I was stunned, but everyone who knew me and my songs looked over at me and clearly knew what was happening. At that very moment, hearing her sing my song to a room filled with thousands of people was so overwhelming, that the silliness of being worried about where I was sitting melted away as I realized the irony of that moment. My amazement at what I was hearing was quickly replaced as complete embarrassment rushed over me. I literally started to cringe thinking about how ridiculous my thoughts were about being seen. What was wrong with me? I really thought I was more mature than that. My thoughts raced, "Seriously Martha? This is how much you trust God? Do you really think God is limited to where you sit in a room? Don't you believe that God can elevate you from anywhere and do whatever He wants to do whether or not you're seen or unseen?" I was so humbled. God used that moment to expose my insecurities and it was the test I didn't know I needed. Humility was needed *in me* in order for God to do more *for me*.

After the service, people were so excited to find out that the song the guest speaker sang, *Say The Name* was on my latest album, that we sold out of every CD we had at our merch table. To add to that blessing, the conference host invited us to come back and sing again for the second night of the conference! Since we were out of CDs, we drove several hours back home to restock and drove back for the rest of the conference.

Throughout the years, God has used the experience of me sitting inconspicuously behind a wall in a choir stand to show me that none of this is about me, it's all about Jesus. The enemy is so subtle with how He can tempt us to focus on ourselves. The only thing I need to be focused on is the prayer found in John 3:30, "I must decrease so He can increase."

This is a spiritual value that is being lost in our culture today. People are very self-centered and self-obsessed like never before. Everybody clamors to discover, "How can I become wealthy, rich, and famous?" How do I get more likes and followers on social media? The more we focus on ourselves the more threatened, vulnerable, and insecure we become. We look happy and confident but actually we're afraid and hurting. Many people in ministry suffer from an addiction to their specialness, including me. They (we) have an underlying insecurity of being rejected that's driven by fear.

I was afraid of being overlooked and when I was asked to move out of my VIP seat, it felt like rejection and it triggered my unhealed self-esteem issues. With one moment of disappointment my confidence plummeted. I was so quickly knocked off center with a small request that seemed so big to me. I questioned if I mattered when it was my actual job to encourage people to see that only Jesus matters! Have you heard the phrase, "you had one job?!" It's a phrase people use when someone is frustrated that someone has failed at a task they were responsible for, especially when that task seems very easy. That was me! I had one job and that was to lead people to Jesus but instead I was making it all about me.

Keep a right spirit and a good attitude when you are tempted with frustration, and when you do, God will open doors that you could never open for yourself!

In Psalm 51:10 (NIV), the psalmist David cried, "Create in me a clean heart, O God, and renew a right spirit within me."

Your heart is the center of your being, and from your heart, flow all of your feelings and thoughts. My heart was telling me something that wasn't true, my thoughts believed it, and my feelings responded to it. The only way for me to change my thoughts was to renew my mind and change my heart.

Renewal of your mind is a transformation of the way you think and the way you live. Real change happens when we spend time in God's word. When we worship God and spend time in His word, the Holy Spirit illuminates what needs to be transformed and renewed in us, and has the power to change us. To put it simply, the word of God corrects us and tells us to get right, rebukes us and tells us what's not right, and trains us and shows us how to stay right!

If you're hurt or disappointed because you feel overlooked or rejected, remember this: God has not forgotten

Scan to download the song from this chapter.

you and He will never fail you. He has placed gifts and abilities inside of you, and He will use you in ways bigger than you can imagine. Stay humble, remain faithful, and be obedient to what God has called you to do. Keep a right spirit and a good attitude when you are tempted with frustration, and when you do, God will open doors that you could never open for yourself!

PRAYER:

Lord, create in me a pure heart and renew a right spirit within me. Make me aware of the areas in my life that are unhealed. Give me strength to overcome my emotions when I am feeling insecure and overlooked. My worth does not come from myself or anything I've accomplished, but it is in You. Help me to stay humble, obedient, and faithful to whatever You want me to do, go wherever You want me to go, and use me in any way You desire. I submit my will to Your will and thank you in advance for the doors of opportunity you will open in my future as I keep my eyes on you. In Jesus' name, amen.

NINE

I KNOW THE PLANS

♪

I know the plans I have for you
I know just what you're
   going through
So when you can't see
What tomorrow holds
And yesterday is through
Remember, I know
The plans I have for you

To give you hope for tomorrow
Joy for your sorrow
Strength for everything
   you go through
Remember, I know the
   plans I have for you

MUSIC AND LYRICS BY MARTHA MUNIZZI

"For I know the plans I have for you," declares
the Lord, "plans to prosper you and not to harm
you, plans to give you hope and a future."
—JEREMIAH 29:11 (NIV)

Have you ever been in a season of your life that you loved? You really enjoyed it, and it felt comfortable to you? Maybe you finally found a job, a church, or a friendship group that fulfilled you on a deep level. Only now, it appears as if God is requiring you to lay it down and walk away. Jeremiah 29:11 is one of my favorite scriptures in the Bible. I love it for many reasons, but one of the main reasons is because it represents a massive turning point in my life and in the life of my family.

My husband, Dan, and I had been serving in our church as worship leaders, and after eight years, we started feeling a pull to step away. We didn't want to go. We had been asking God to do greater things in us and through us, and we were feeling drawn to travel more and minister outside of church. However, we never thought God was requiring a total surrender of a place where we had found so much fulfillment. It was not an easy transition. In fact, it was one of the hardest seasons of our lives. It required more trust and sacrifice than I ever thought possible. I remember one Sunday night after church. We had just said our final goodbyes to all of our friends—the people we had built a community with for eight years—and I was hurting. I couldn't understand why God required this. The big "Why?" was the only thing I could ask God.

Transitions are hard because you have to let go of one thing to take hold of the next. You have to let go of comfort and what's familiar and safe to go after all that God has. In transition seasons, there's often not a lot of clarity. The only thing you're sure of is that one season is ending. You have no idea what the next season holds or when it will start. And now, after I was sitting in a room in my home crying out to God, asking Him, "Why?" and "What's next?", it was hard to imagine our lives better or more exciting than what we had experienced in those eight years. "God!" I sobbed, "I know you spoke to us about stepping out in faith, and we did it. Just promise me you didn't bring me out here into 'no man's land' to leave me! Promise me that you have something greater for me to do. I'll do whatever you ask. All I want is for you to use my life for your glory!"

I had my Bible on my lap, and as tears fell down my face, I opened my Bible, and it fell open to Jeremiah 29:11. I promise that is exactly what happened! I would never make that up! When I read it, I cried even more! I was still scared, but I knew it was a promise from God for me in that very moment. God had a plan! I had no idea what, why, when, or how, but I knew God was speaking to me. A melody came to my mind, so I started singing the words of the scripture to the melody I was hearing. The song flowed out so quickly and easily, and every word and note gave me so much comfort. From then on, I started singing it everywhere I went.

> *God began to open small doors for us that eventually led to bigger doors of opportunity. God had a plan all along! A plan that was bigger and better than anything I could have ever imagined! He has a plan for you, too.*

God began to open small doors for us that eventually led to bigger doors of opportunity. God had a plan all along! A plan that was bigger and better than anything I could have ever imagined! He has a plan for you, too. Think about this: God's plan for you is very specific. The definition of the word plan is "to decide on and arrange in advance," according to the *Oxford English Dictionary*.[4] God's plan has already been arranged and decided. He's not making it up as He goes along. He

---

4 "Plan English Definition and Meaning," *Lexico Dictionaries | English*, https://www.lexico.com/en/definition/plan.

is a God who is strategic with the plan He has for your life. Ephesians 2:10 (NIV) says, "For we are God's handiwork, created in Christ Jesus to do good works, which God prepared in advance for us to do." This doesn't sound like God is winging it. His plan for your life has been well thought out and prepared so that you can fulfill His destiny for your life and do good works! You have work to do! There is kingdom purpose waiting for you to fulfill it.

God has a plan to prosper you. God's plan is for you to flourish—not just financially but in your life and in your health. Your health matters to God! Your strength matters to God! Isaiah 54:17 (BSB) promises that "No weapon formed against you shall prosper" He won't let anything from the enemy that might work against you prosper. It can't succeed, flourish, or grow!

His plan is for you to have a future and a hope. Something in the future happens in a time to come. In other words, IT WILL HAPPEN! God's plan for your life will manifest! And not only will He give you a future that will flourish and prosper, but He will give you hope if you just trust Him. Hebrews 11:1 (NIV) says, "Now faith is confidence in what we hope for and assurance about what we do not see." Trusting God and taking a giant leap of faith into the unknown is scary. You will have to deal with fear, insecurity, and waiting. Learn to believe in the unseen. Faith is confidence in what we can't see. We believe it, but we can't see it yet. If you're believing God for a promise that you're still waiting on, hope will come when you verbalize your faith. Praise and thanksgiving are verbalized faith. Thanking God after the prayer is answered is called gratitude.

Thanking God before something happens exercises your faith. Hope is a feeling of expectation and desire for a certain thing to happen. Therefore, when Isaiah 40:31(NIV) promises, "But those who hope in the Lord will renew their strength," it is telling God's people to not lose hope! It doesn't matter how long you have to wait—wait, and don't

Scan to download the song from this chapter.

lose hope! Hope deferred makes the heart sick! God wants you well and whole!

I have learned through the process of waiting that delay is not denial! In fact, the longer the wait, the greater the miracle! Don't be discouraged by what you see now. Put your hope in the Lord, and trust that He has a plan! Greater days are coming!

PRAYER

Father, I thank You today that You have a plan for my life. Help me let go of all the pain and disappointments of yesterday and reach towards the future by faith. Help me see with eyes of faith the greater plan You have for me. God, Your plan for me is greater than anything I can dream for myself, and I will be full of hope and expectation for the favor and miracles You have planned for my future! In Jesus's name. Amen.

TEN

" MAKE IT LOUD "

♪

Make it big, make it loud
Shout it all around the world
All around the world
Let the people celebrate
Celebrate Jesus!

No other God can save,
(like our God)
No other God can heal,
(like our God)
No other God can deliver,
(like our God)
No other God can set us
free, (like our God)

So we rejoice and sing
We celebrate our king
We are not ashamed
Everybody

Make it big, make it loud
Shout it all around the world
All around the world
Let the people celebrate
Make it big, make it loud
Shout it all around the world
All around the world
Celebrate Jesus!

MUSIC AND LYRICS BY MARTHA MUNIZZI

I n 2008, the song "I Kissed a Girl and I Liked It," written and performed by Katy Perry, a very famous pop star, became the #1 song in the world. Initially, the song sparked controversy, but in retrospect, it has been viewed as the beginning of LGBTQ awareness in pop music. The song topped the U.S. Billboard Hot 100 chart for seven consecutive weeks, becoming the "1,000[th] #1 song of the Rock era."[5] The single has sold six million units in the U.S. alone, according to the Recording Industry Association of America.[6] It also topped the charts in Australia, Austria, Belgium, Canada, the Czech Republic, Denmark, Germany, Hungary, Ireland, Italy, New Zealand, Norway, Scotland, Sweden, Switzerland, and the United Kingdom. It was the bestselling song of 2008 in Finland. The song has been certified multi-platinum in Australia, Canada, Denmark, the UK, and the US.

I was shocked and troubled when I heard the song. At the time, my daughters were a lot younger, and I knew instantly this song was going to shape our culture in a destructive way and open the door to confusion in the lives of young people all over the world. I got mad— mad that the enemy was so brazen and bold. I realized after I prayed about it that I didn't have to react in my emotions. I just needed to continue to do what God's Word tells me to do and keep praising God. I didn't have to shout and yell about what the enemy was doing; all I needed to do was give God even more praise! The enemy has already been defeated, so no matter how loud the lies of the enemy become, I just need to get louder with my praise.

When circumstances look dire, don't waste your energy worrying about what the enemy is doing. Be more concerned with what God is doing. Your problem needs your praise! Can you make it loud when the enemy's voice is screaming lies and confusion? Can you make it loud when the voices of fear, worry, and failure threaten to drown out your praise?

When I had just started traveling, I was invited to lead worship at a women's conference. I was beyond excited to debut my new songs

---

5 "I Kissed a Girl by Katy Perry," *Songfacts*, https://www.songfacts.com/facts/katy-perry/i-kissed-a-girl.
6 "Gold & Platinum," *RIAA*, https://www.riaa.com/gold-platinum/?tab_active=default-award&ar=KATY%2BPERRY.

as well as honored to be a special guest at this event. When I arrived for the third night of the conference, I was ushered through a crowd of very excited women. I sat down right next to the first lady of the church. "First Lady" is the title of honor for the lead pastor's wife of many African-American churches.

> *When circumstances look dire, don't waste your energy worrying about what the enemy is doing. Be more concerned with what God is doing. Your problem needs your praise! Make it loud when the enemy's voice is screaming lies and confusion, and the voices of fear, worry, and failure threaten to drown out your praise.*

The worship team had just started singing the first song, so most of us were still getting positioned in our places and setting our purses down; many were not fully focused on the worship at this point. I remember looking around and smiling at the beautiful women in the room. Once I focused on the worship, I noticed a young woman on the platform who was a member of the choir. She was dancing and leaping around, but she was—for the most part—maintaining her space in her section in the choir stand. It distracted me for a moment, but I looked away and tried to stay focused on the worship.

A few seconds later, the woman began to sing so loudly that she was on the verge of becoming a disturbance. She soon ramped up from dancing and singing to shouting and yelling! Then she came out of the choir and onto the main stage. She was jumping and spinning, and no one was stopping her! It was obvious to me that she was "out of order" and had become a major distraction in the worship service. I remember thinking, *Someone should stop her! Where are the leaders who should have taught her and trained her properly? Why are they allowing her to bring so much attention to herself? The pastor or the first lady should do something because I can't worship with all of this chaos!*

As my judgmental thoughts persisted, they were interrupted suddenly when the first lady leaned over to me and whispered in my ear. "Do you see that woman on the stage doing all that jumping and shouting?" "Yes!" I whispered back. It was pretty obvious that everyone could see AND hear her. The first lady leaned over again and said, "A few days ago she lost her newborn baby. She's been praising God like that ever since. She made the choice to keep praising God even in her pain and grief. She has not stopped singing and shouting, and it has impacted our church so much that we have been experiencing a move of God ever since!"

My face burned with embarrassment. Gutted is the only word to describe how I felt. I should have known better. God used that experience to humble me and knock me down a few pegs. I needed it! Never judge the way someone worships. Of course, discernment matters because there are some people who might take advantage, but it's better to err on the side of giving people freedom in their expression to worship.

This grieving mother chose to worship in the middle of her pain! I saw it as her creating chaos, but she saw it as her only way of survival. She had to get loud to overcome the suffering she was going through, and she didn't care what anyone else thought about her. Her loud, exuberant praise was healing her broken heart and breaking chains in the atmosphere.

The story of the children of Israel is that of a nation dealing with pain and chaos, desperately trying to survive. They lived through four hundred years of slavery in Egypt, and after generations of bondage, Moses had negotiated their freedom from the grip of Pharaoh and his army. The Israelites were running for their lives. I can imagine the desperation of the exodus of over two million families, hoping and praying for their long-awaited miracle, expecting God to do something mighty! I can just imagine Moses' sister Miriam feverishly packing to escape with her people. As she frantically packed whatever belongings she could take with her, she made sure to pack her tambourine. I think it's because she had experienced God's deliverance in the past and was expecting a victory in the future.

Exodus 15:19-21 (NIV) describes:

When Pharaoh's horses, chariots and horsemen went into the sea, the Lord brought the waters of the sea back over them, but the Israelites walked through the sea on dry ground. Then Miriam the prophet, Aaron's sister, took a timbrel in her hand, and all the women followed her, with timbrels and dancing. Miriam sang to them:

"Sing to the Lord, for he is highly exalted. Both horse and driver he has hurled into the sea."

She thought ahead to the victory that was coming, and she was ready for war. Even in the chaos of the moment, she remembered to pack her tambourine. What does a tambourine have to do with being loud in our praise? Have you ever played a tambourine? It's one of the easiest instruments to play, and it cuts through the noise with a distinctively sharp sound. I've recorded eight live albums and have enforced a "no tambourine" rule when we're recording. Tambourines are banned from the room because it doesn't matter how loud every other instrument is, whether it's keyboards, guitar, or drums, the tambourine cuts through them all. Many live recordings have been disrupted by somebody in the audience shaking a tambourine.

Miriam didn't need that tambourine just for the victory dance. It was her weapon of warfare, too.

The Bible shows us that praise will defeat our enemies. Second Chronicles 20:22 (NIV) says, "As they began to sing and praise, the Lord set ambushes against the men of Ammon and Moab and Mount Seir who were invading Judah, and they were defeated."

Praise is not only the pursuit of God's presence; it is an instrument of war. It blocks the spiritual attack that creates suffering, turmoil, strife, and confusion. Praise destroys the atmosphere in which sickness, disease, and discouragement flourish. Praise stops the enemy where he stands and ushers in the presence of God.

The enemy's voice acts as a barrier between us and heaven, just like air molecules create a barrier between layers of the atmosphere. When that natural barrier—the sound barrier—is broken, it makes a sound called a "sonic boom." To break the sound barrier, a plane's nose pushes through the air's resistance by thrusting forward. As the plane begins to break the barrier, water vapor and pressure move to the tail of the craft. As full penetration occurs, the barrier of resistance explodes, and the catalyst of sonic thrust causes the plane to catapult forward, slamming all of those air molecules together to create what is known in science as a sonic boom. In other words, whatever resistance is keeping the plane from moving forward, becomes the thrust that is needed to catapult it forward.

Leading up to sonic boom level, though, at any time, the pilot can release the pressure by decreasing speed and falling back where it's comfortable and predictable. Or he can thrust forward to where few have gone before and BREAK THROUGH into the sonic boom level.

We are faced with the same choices in our praise.

Is there a situation in your life that is intimidating you?

Scan to download the song from this chapter.

Is there a voice in your head that is threatening your position of victory? Amplify your voice louder than the voice of your enemy. Make your praise big, make it loud, and shout it all around the world! Celebrate Jesus, and drown out the voice of the enemy with your own sonic boom of praise!

PRAYER

*Dear Heavenly Father, there is no other God
like You—I praise You for the great works
of Your hands. You alone can save, heal,
deliver, and set me free from the bondage
of the enemy. Today, I will not shrink back
or give You a half-hearted praise. Use me
to bring hope and love to the people around
me, and fill me with joy, so I can shout
from the top of my lungs how great and
wonderful You are! In Jesus's name. Amen.*

ELEVEN

SAY THE NAME

♪

Say the name of Jesus,
say the name of Jesus
Say the name of Jesus,
no other name I know
Say the name of Jesus,
say the name of Jesus
Say the name of Jesus,
no other name I know

That can calm your fears
    and dry your tears
And wipe away your pain
When you don't know
    what else to pray
When you don't know
    what else to say
Say the name

Jesus, Jesus
Jesus, Jesus
Jesus, Jesus
Jesus, Jesus

He's gonna make a way
    when you say
When you don't know
    what else to pray
When you don't know
    what else to say
When you can't make it
    through another day
Say the name

MUSIC AND LYRICS BY MARTHA MUNIZZI

I 'll never forget the moment God gave me this song. I was sitting in a parking lot in a car with our three children, waiting for my husband to get off work. The kids were strapped into their car seats, excitedly anticipating Daddy taking us home. I was tired from a long day and ready to get home, but I was also happy that nobody was fighting in the back seat. Just as I was about to get frustrated from waiting for Dan, I had a thought: *I really need to write a song about the name of Jesus.* I don't know why the Holy Spirit interrupted my thoughts at that particular time, but I'm thankful He did!

Out of nowhere, the lyrics and the melody began to pour out: *Say the name of Jesus. Say the name of Jesus. Say the name so precious . . . no other name I know.* I knew something amazing was happening and that a song from heaven was being downloaded into my heart. At the same time that this God moment was happening, my kids decided to take playing to the next level and started fighting. I was literally having a supernatural experience with God, and in the middle of it, I had to turn around and discipline my kids!

"Mommy is getting a song from God!" I yelled. It was not one of my best moments, but what do you do when you're right in between the super and the natural? God was speaking to me, and my kids were fighting! The only thing I could do was try not to freak out. Honestly, sometimes that's all you can do! God will show up in the crazy chaos and bless you beyond your ability to comprehend it. Sometimes, God will choose a moment that you are not expecting to show up in your life. He'll choose a time in your life that won't be convenient to do the unexpected. God will show up at a time that could be your greatest moment of loss and give you your greatest victory.

What have I learned? BLESSINGS AND BATTLES CAN OCCUR AT THE SAME TIME.

Several years ago, after I had recorded my live album *No Limits*, my husband and I went on tour and decided to take our children with us. Our youngest, Nathan, was eight years old at the time, and he was so excited to go on a long trip with us. We rented a large tour bus and were looking forward to traveling with our new music all over the country. Our first booking was at one of the largest Christian TV networks in the U.S. We were scheduled that evening to go on LIVE broadcasting to millions of people all over the country. We knew God had given us this opportunity to have so many people hear our new music.

We drove into town earlier that day and checked into our hotel. Our daughters, Danielle and Nicole, were in an adjoining room while Nathan stayed with us to rest and get ready for the broadcast that night. I remember lying down to rest before getting ready, and Nathan came and got in bed with Dan and I. I thought it was strange because eight-year-old boys rarely take naps in the middle of the day. I tried to sleep, but I couldn't get settled. I kept looking over at Nathan, who was asleep with his back to me. I started feeling really troubled and anxious about something, but I couldn't put my finger on what was bothering me. Before I could even pray and ask God what was troubling me, Nathan turned in my direction. To my surprise he was having a full-blown seizure! He had never had a seizure before, and I started to panic!

"What's happening? Dan! Nathan is having a seizure!" My husband jumped up out of a deep sleep and started to panic himself. I realized we didn't both need to get upset, so I tried my best to stay calm. I called 911, and while we waited for the ambulance to come, I did the only thing I could think of doing: I started to sing, *Say the name of Jesus. When you don't know what else to say, when you can't find the words to say, say the name. Jesus! He's gonna make a way when you say Jesus!*

I sang it over and over, even after Nathan stopped seizing. I sang it in the hospital room with Nathan while waiting for the results of the tests they conducted to find out where the seizure had come from. At one point, I was sitting next to Nathan in his hospital bed, and I stopped singing to rest for a minute and to pray. I prayed, "God, I'm asking you to heal Nathan of whatever is causing this, and I declare that he will never have another seizure for the rest of his life in the name of Jesus!" Nathan said, "Mommy, don't stop singing. I'm scared, and the only time I feel peace is when you sing." I kept singing until he fell asleep.

A few minutes later, the doctor came in and said the tests were all negative. They couldn't find anything that would cause a seizure. We praised God all the way back to the hotel room! That night, on LIVE television, we shared Nathan's testimony of how the enemy tried to intimidate us, but the name of Jesus is more powerful! Nathan is now twenty-five years old and has never had another seizure to this day! God answers prayer! Today, I encourage you to use the name of Jesus over every circumstance. The power and authority of the name of Jesus belongs to you as a born-again believer, and He expects you to use it!

> *There is a force so vast in its power that it triumphs over any problem, any trial, and any situation. Demons flee from it, disease cannot remain in the face of it, lack and fear dissipate before it, and darkness is instantly shattered by it. Even death itself cannot contend with it. What is it? It's the Name above all names—the name of Jesus.*

Matthew 28:18 (NIV) says, "Before Jesus ascended to be seated at the right hand of the Father, He said, 'All authority in heaven and on earth has been given to me.'" Jesus has all authority! There is a force so vast in its power that it triumphs over any problem, any trial, and any situation. Demons flee from it, disease cannot remain in the face of it, lack and fear dissipate before it, and darkness is instantly shattered by it. Even death itself cannot contend with it. What is it? It's the Name above all names—the name of Jesus.

The power and authority of the name of Jesus rightfully belongs to you as a born-again Christian, and He expects you to use it! What did He do with it? He entrusted it to us when He said:

> "Go into all the world and preach the gospel to every creature. . . . And these signs will follow those who believe: In My name they will cast out demons; they will speak with new tongues; they will take up serpents; and if they drink anything deadly, it will by no means hurt them; they will lay hands on the sick, and they will recover."
> —Mark 16:15 and 17-18 (NKJV)

The name of Jesus works. There is far more power wrapped up in those two syllables than you realize. Smith Wigglesworth once said, "There is power to overcome everything in the world through the name of Jesus."[7] That means you can put the name of Jesus to work in every area of your life—big or small. Below are four instances when you should use the name of Jesus.

1) Use the name of Jesus to put sickness to flight.

> "In my name . . . they will lay hands on the sick, and they will recover."
> —MARK 16:17-18 (NKJV)

---

7 Smith Wigglesworth, "The Power of the name," *Smith Wigglesworth*, http://www.smithwigglesworth.com/index.php/smith-wigglesworth-sermons/ever-increasing-faith/the-power-of-the-name.

Healing is God's calling card. If you learn to use the name of Jesus, you won't have any trouble getting people saved. It is the easiest thing in the world to get people saved when you get them healed first. Jump-start your faith by using the name of Jesus.

2) Use the name of Jesus to rebuke lack.

Therefore, God elevated him to the place of highest
honor and gave him the name above all other names,
that at the name of Jesus every knee should bow,
in heaven and on earth and under the earth.
—Philippians 2:9-10 (NIV)

Just like every sickness has a name, lack is a name, and it covers more than money. Any area where you are in lack—peace in your family, joy in your spirit, finances in your life—has to bow to the name of Jesus. Stand your ground in every area.

3) Use the name of Jesus to send demons away.

"In My name, they will cast out demons."
—Mark 16:17 (NKJV)

Have you ever noticed that the devil doesn't play fair? Well, God never told you to give the devil a fair shot either—He said to use the name of Jesus on him because he's already defeated! You have authority over the spirits of strife, envy, suicide, murder, drugs, alcoholism, or any other wrong spirit that tries to enter your home and family. Deal with it IMMEDIATELY! Speak to it. Say, "I command you in Jesus's name to take your hands off my children. You spirit of rebellion, drugs, alcohol (whatever it is), I break your power over my child, my spouse, and my family. I forbid you to operate in his or her life anymore. I take by force what belongs to me, and that includes my children and my family. You get out in Jesus's name!" If you even smell the devil from a distance, roaming and trying to break into any area of your life, don't wait for it to escalate—get him out! And do it with the Name above all names.

4) Use the name of Jesus for supernatural protection.

The name of the Lord is a strong fortress; the
godly run to him and are safe.
—PROVERBS 18:10 (NLT)

My Nana, Dorothy Arnold, born in 1917, was the daughter of a carnival man. When she was a teenager, her father relocated the family to Florida, hoping that the temperature would be more favorable for her mother's health. Soon after Nana enrolled in the local high school, her mother passed. Having no church affiliation, a new friend she met reached out, who went to a local Full Gospel Church. As a result, she was saved and filled with the Spirit. All throughout her life, including being married for 60 years and raising four children, she would tell stories of supernatural, divine intervention. In one particular story, she described an event that happened a few years before she passed at 93 years old. She went to the local Walmart and upon exiting, she couldn't remember where she parked her car. She ventured out, thinking she was headed in the right direction when a gentleman came alongside her with a very pleasant and calming tone and said, "let me help you." She was shocked at how natural it seemed but as he led the way, within just a few short steps, there was her car. She was amazed, and when she turned to thank the gentleman, he was gone! The next day, she listened to a news report about a woman who was assaulted at that same Walmart parking lot at the same time she was looking for her car. She always believed that it was divine intervention and her "angel" had protected her. I never doubted after hearing about her encounter that this was an angel. Nana was very

Scan to download the song from this chapter.

pragmatic and kept a sweet skepticism about her most of the time. And if Nana said she encountered a angel...she encountered an angel! Her experience impacted my faith to believe in the supernatural even as a young girl. My own children have heard us tell the story of Nana's encounter with a real angel many times.

> *Saying the name of Jesus should always be your first line of defense and will help you when there seems to be no way out.*

The Bible teaches us that angels are our "protectors" who battle the enemies of God's people both seen and unseen.

Psalm 34:7 (NIV) summarizes it this way, "The angel of the Lord encamps around those who fear him, and he delivers them."

I don't know about you, but I'm so glad we have these angelic warriors on our side, guiding us, protecting us, and warring for us!

The name of Jesus is your supernatural protection, your emergency number, and your rescue vehicle all wrapped up in one. It responds immediately, acts perfectly, and gets the job done without delay or hiccup. Saying the name of Jesus should always be your first line of defense and will help you when there seems to be no way out. There is power in the name of Jesus. When you don't know what else to say . . . say His name! Begin to speak it with confidence and authority. It's a mighty weapon of warfare that never fails!

PRAYER

Jesus, thank You for the power in Your mighty name. Your name is all I need. Your name is above every name, and when I speak the name of Jesus, demons have to flee. Sickness has to go. Poverty has to go. Lack has to go. When I say the name of Jesus, I am healed and whole. Today, I will speak the name of Jesus over my family, my finances, and my future.

Jesus, I thank You that I have authority in Your mighty name! I speak the name of Jesus over my loved ones, and I rebuke sickness, lack, and any other demonic spirit trying to infiltrate my family. Jesus, I thank You for supernatural protection that covers me everywhere I go. I speak blessing over my life in every area, in the powerful name of Jesus! Amen.

TWELVE

WE SAY YES

♪

*Every promise He has
  given is yes, is yes
Every whisper He has
  spoken is yes, is yes
I am confident in every
  word He said
He is faithful to complete
  what He began
All the promises of God
  are stamped with*

*Yes, Amen
Yes, Amen*

*Every stronghold will be
  broken with yes, with yes
We, your people, won't
  be shaken—we say
  yes, we say yes
I am confident in every
  word He said
He is faithful to complete
  what He began*

*All the promises of God
  are stamped with*

*Yes, we are believing
Yes, we are receiving
The promise of your healing
We say yes
Yes to every miracle
Yes to supernatural
The promise we've been
  waiting for
Yes, our God is faithful
Yes, our God is able
His promises unshakable
We say yes
Yes, hell is defeated
Yes, we stand in freedom
The promises of Jesus
We say yes*

*Yes, Amen
Yes, Amen*

MUSIC AND LYRICS BY MARTHA MUNIZZI & ISRAEL HOUGHTON

There are hundreds—possibly thousands—of promises in the Bible for believers. One of my favorite promises is found in Psalm 37:4 (NKJV) "Delight yourself also in the LORD, and He shall give you the desires of your heart."

2 Corinthians 1:20 (NKJV) says, "For all the promises of God in Him are Yes, and in Him Amen, to the glory of God through us." When God's promises are fulfilled in our lives, it brings God glory!

The message translation says it this way, "Whatever God has promised gets stamped with the Yes of Jesus. In him, this is what we preach and pray, the great Amen, God's Yes and our Yes together, gloriously evident. God affirms us, making us a sure thing in Christ, putting his Yes within us. By his Spirit he has stamped us with his eternal pledge—a sure beginning of what he is destined to complete."

In the book of Numbers is the story of the Israelites who were about to step into the promised land. Moses sent twelve spies into the land to spy it out and bring back a report and see what it would take to conquer it for God's people. Out of twelve spies, only two came back with a good report. Only two out of twelve believed and trusted in God's promises. Those two men were Caleb and Joshua.

Numbers 13:30 (NIV) describes: "Then Caleb silenced the people before Moses and said, " We should go up and take possession of the land, for we can certainly do it." Caleb said, "Let's go get it!" I love this about Caleb because he understood that if God said they could do it then they could do it!

The Israelites had a vision: Get to the promised land! That's why they left Egypt; however, along the way, things didn't always go their way and many began to lose their excitement for the vision set before them. The vision is clear, but how you carry yourself in the process of seeing the vision become a reality always matters more!

If vision is where we are going, culture is how we get there. The issue for Israel was that they allowed their obstacles, their fears, and their insecurities to become the dominant culture in their lives. When the spies went to investigate the Promised Land, most of them came back saying the people were too strong, the obstacles too big, and the cities too large to overcome.

Caleb knew there was a culture that comes with being God's people. We have to have a culture that's full of faith!

What is culture? Culture is a way of life for a group of people--the behaviors, beliefs, values, and symbols that they accept, generally without thinking about them. What is your faith culture? What are your behaviors and beliefs? What are you accepting without thinking? Has a specific mindset become the norm without you ever challenging your thoughts and ideas? I believe it's time to stop holding on to our wrong beliefs and start searching for the truth! The truth is, God's yes is waiting for our yes! His promises are already bought and paid for by the precious blood of Jesus. And we've been given the Holy Spirit as our guarantee that what God has promised will absolutely come to pass!

Hebrews 11:1 (NKJV) "Now faith is the substance of things hoped for, the evidence of things not seen," and Hebrews 11:3 (NLT) says, "By faith we understand that the entire universe was formed at God's command, that what we now see did not come from anything that can be seen."

Caleb and Joshua knew they must live their lives by faith in God's promises, and because of that they were able to enter the Promised Land. Where the other spies and the rest of Israel confessed negativity and defeat, Caleb and Joshua confessed victory. If you don't want to be like the ten spies, don't confess the way they did, because your confession will frame your reality.

If you could confront any of the ten spies about their negative report, they'd say, "Hey, we're just keeping it real. We're just calling it like we see it."

What made Caleb and Joshua say something completely different when all twelve witnessed the same thing? They chose to believe what God had promised, in spite of the evidence in front of their eyes:

"The land we passed through and explored is exceedingly good. If the LORD is pleased with us, he will lead us into that land, a land flowing with milk and honey, and will give it to us. Only do not rebel against the LORD. And do not be afraid of the people of the land, because we will devour them. Their protection is gone, but the LORD is with us. Do not be afraid of them." —Numbers 14:7-9 (NIV)

What a great spirit Caleb and Joshua had; where there's a will, there's a way! Look at the contrasting perspectives. Group one said, "If the Lord would. . . .then we could." The other says, "The Lord will, SO WE WILL!!" The big difference is that the 'would' culture takes no responsibility while the 'will' culture takes faith.

Because the people couldn't get in alignment with what God wanted to do, that generation of Israelites didn't inherit what God had promised. Their lack of faith completely shaped the history of Israel. They spent the next forty years wandering in the desert instead of experiencing the power and faithfulness of God in the Promised Land.

In Numbers 13:30. Caleb said, "Let us go up at once . . ." He was aggressively engaged in the mission of God. Your "Yes" is time-sensitive. We need to, in faith, be aggressive. God wants us to take ground for His kingdom, not sit back and be satisfied with what we have. God wants us to see the "big armies" and get excited about how He will move them out of the way. We're not aggressive based on what 'we' can do, but we are moving forward aggressively because we know what 'God' can do and what He's promised to do!

Caleb and Joshua stood their ground. Nobody around them believed it could be done, but that didn't change Caleb and Joshua's conviction to move forward. Fear does not advance the kingdom of God—faith does. Don't make decisions out of fear, instead, make them in faith. We need to learn to stand our ground in faith.

Start with saying yes to believing that God is able to do exceedingly, abundantly, above all we could ever ask or think. Say yes to whatever God is asking you to do. Your yes is all God needs to fulfill every one of His promises to you!

Hebrews 4:2 (NKJV) explains about the people of Israel, "For indeed the gospel was preached to us as well as to them; but the word which they heard did not profit them, not being mixed with faith in those who heard it."

The children of God heard His word and promises, but they didn't receive anything from God because they didn't combine what they heard with faith. They never obtained what God promised them because they walked in unbelief instead of faith.

Faith is believing that you already have what you're hoping for; it's pulling God's promises from the spirit realm into the physical realm.

God puts His promises out there for anyone who will receive.

Those who believe in faith that God is Who He says He is and that He'll do what He said He'll do—no matter what the circumstances around them look like—they believe and obey anyway.

Start with saying yes to believing that God is able to

Scan to download the song from this chapter.

do exceedingly, abundantly, above all we could ever ask or think. Say yes to whatever God is asking you to do. Your "Yes" is all God needs to fulfill every one of His promises to you!

PRAYER

*God, I thank You for the calling and vision You
have placed on my life. Give me the strength
to say yes to that vision and do what you
are calling me to do. I pray that my actions
serve Your vision and that my words resonate
with the vision of my leaders. Help me to be
a bold leader and confront mediocrity. Holy
Spirit, please teach me to live a lifestyle of
excellence and to put my heart and soul into
everything I do. Help me to be faithful with
the little and know that it is preparing me for
the more You have for me. Help me to continue
to sow into and be faithful in the season
I find myself. I trust that You are working all
things out for the good of those who love You
and are called according to your purpose.*

I choose today to align my confession with the promises of Your word. I choose to bring a culture of faith into every environment. I choose, when times get tough, to remember your goodness and your grace. I pray that the desires You have for me will become the desires of my heart. Lead me into all of Your incredible plans and promises for my life. In Jesus' name, Amen.

THIRTEEN

HEAVEN

♪

I wanna see heaven,
heaven on earth
I wanna see heaven,
heaven on earth

I wanna see miracles,
miracles on earth
I wanna see Jesus,
I wanna see Jesus

MUSIC AND LYRICS BY MARTHA MUNIZZI, DAVID OUTING, LEONARD RAY JARMAN JR

My parents were traveling evangelists when I was growing up. They would travel to churches all over the U.S., and my mother would play the piano and sing with my father right before he would preach. Most of the time, my sisters and I would go with them, but three toddlers under the age of four was a challenge, so my parents would sometimes leave us with a family member or trusted babysitter for a couple of days.

My twin sister, Mary, and I were only a year old and were staying with our sitter when I contracted a fever that was over 104 degrees. Because my fever was so high and I was extremely listless, I was rushed to the hospital. My parents waited patiently in the waiting room, and held each other as they listened to the doctor explain that a spinal tap was needed to find out what was wrong. The spinal tap test results came back, and the doctors' worst fears were realized. There was a high probability that I had spinal meningitis. This was a grim diagnosis. My parents were told I had little chance of making it through the night. If by some miracle I did survive, I could possibly be paralyzed for the rest of my life. My parents were devastated.

My father sat next to my hospital bed all night long, praying for a miracle. As he prayed and cried out, God spoke to him, *John, are there any cases of spinal meningitis in heaven?* My dad was puzzled by the question, but then he responded, "No, Lord, there is no spinal meningitis in heaven." My father heard God speak again, *Are there any sick babies in heaven?* My Dad responded again, "No, Lord, there are no sick babies in heaven. The Bible says, 'There will be no more death or mourning or crying or pain.'" God said, *Then this is how I want you to pray: On earth as it is in heaven.* My Father started praying Matthew 6:9-10 (NIV): "Our Father in heaven, hallowed be your name. Your kingdom come, your will be done, on earth as it is in heaven." Dad said he prayed that prayer until the sun came up the next morning!

The very next morning, to the doctor's amazement, I was awake and ready to eat! No fever. No weakness. No evidence of spinal meningitis! Thank You, Jesus! My dad told this story many times as I was growing up, and it has impacted me deeply. I learned that God is a healer, and if we put our faith in Him, He has the power to bring heaven to earth.

In heaven, there are no tears, no complaining, no worrying, no pain, and no sorrow! There is only joy, peace, celebration, and worship around the throne! And when we live a life of worship, we can actually experience heaven on earth and bring heaven down! In heaven, the worship never stops! It's continual praise! And whatever is happening in heaven can happen on earth!

In my song "Heaven," there is a part that says, "Release the sound of victory!" Victory is the sound of heaven! As believers we have the authority to declare victory because death has been defeated. When Jesus died and was resurrected, He won back our victory!

In heaven, there are no tears, no complaining, no worrying, no pain, and no sorrow! There is only joy, peace, celebration, and worship around the throne! And when we live a life of worship, we can actually experience heaven on earth and bring heaven down!

God's plan has always been to bring victory into your story. So, when all hell breaks loose in your life, and you need a miracle from heaven that only God can bring, shout the praises of God, and release the sound of victory in your life. Your worship invites the very presence of God into your situation, and when the Holy Spirit shows up, His power shows up. His love shows up. His joy shows up. Healing shows up. Everything you need shows up when God Himself comes to where you are! Praise God every day, and bring heaven to earth!

Scan to download the song from this chapter.

PRAYER

Lord Jesus, thank You for the privilege of worship. I am honored and grateful to give You the praise You deserve. Today, I will start to look at my situation from heaven's perspective. Give me the ability to trust in You, so I can bring heaven down to earth every day. In Jesus's name. Amen!

FOURTEEN

SHOUT

♪

Shout with a voice of triumph
Shout with a voice of praise
Shout with a voice of triumph
Shout with a voice of praise
Shout unto God for the
*   victory, hey, hey*
Give the Lord a shout of praise

Triumphant in battle,
*   we are victorious*

God is most high over
*   all the earth*
Jesus has conquered,
*   Satan's defeated*
The enemy is under my
*   feet, so I will...*

Shout for the victory
Shout if you've been set free
Shout!

MUSIC AND LYRICS BY MARTHA MUNIZZI

Every worship leader typically has a chosen weeknight to bring their musicians and singers together to rehearse for the upcoming weekend services. Rehearsal is a great time to build relationships and comradery with the members of the music team, as well as learn new worship songs for Sundays. During one of our choir rehearsals years ago, I wanted to teach our choir and worship band a new song I had just written. I was nervous because being a new songwriter I wasn't sure if it was good. I had sung it for my husband,

Dan, and he liked it, so even though I was insecure about it, I decided to sing it for my team.

If you've ever worked with singers and musicians before, you know how the learning process can go. It can be a humbling and excruciating experience, introducing a brand-new song. It's a hot mess before it all comes together! When no one knows the lyrics, and they haven't figured out their part to sing, it can sound like a train wreck. The key is to not give up on the song or the team until you've spent enough time rehearsing until all the parts start coming together. Trust me; it's easy to get discouraged at the sound of singers clamoring to find their parts or musicians fiddling on their instruments trying to find the right notes to play.

Once everyone had learned their parts, I heard the song come together for the first time. It sounded so bad I wanted to throw out the new song and get rid of the team altogether! I was really hoping that once it came together and I heard the lyrics and harmonies gel, I would feel better about it. On the contrary, I hated it even more. I went from being unsure if it was a good song, to being convinced I had written the worst song that had ever been written in the history of music! (I was a little dramatic back when I was younger.) That was it for me! I decided right then and there that this song would never see the light of day. How could I have ever thought it was good?

I started to question my song-writing ability. I remember thinking, *Who do you think you are? Where did you get the idea that you could write songs? You need to stick to singing and stay in your lane.* (I told you I was dramatic, right?) After that night, I pretended as if that rehearsal had never happened and threw out my new song. Weeks went by, and I had forgotten all about it until one of my choir members, born and raised in North Carolina, came up to me, and with the biggest Southern drawl I had ever heard, said to me, "Hey, Martha, why haven't we sung that new song you wrote?"

"What song?" I asked.

"That song you taught us a few weeks ago about shouting with a voice of triumph," she said. (I think she started her sentence with "Bless your heart," which is a Southerner's way of saying, "You're an idiot," without outright saying it.)

I looked at her, stunned, and said, "You liked that song? I threw it away because I thought it was stupid."

She looked back at me with fire in her eyes and said, "That song isn't stupid. You're stupid!"

She had a great sense of humor which she was using to make her point, and we both started laughing. She was right! I *was* being stupid. Because of my insecurity, I had thrown away something God had given me. I started working on the song again. I changed the key and added a few verses, and the song "Shout" was born! It became one of our church's favorite songs, has gone on to be recorded by gospel great Alvin Slaughter as well as several other artists, and is regularly on the set list at Lakewood Church in Houston, Texas.

The enemy didn't want that song to be birthed because of its message. He fed me lies of inadequacy and insecurity to make me doubt the gift God had given me. I had to get set free of the very thing the song talked about!

The word praise is the Hebrew word *shabach*. *Shabach* means "to shout, to address in a loud tone, to command, to triumph."[8] This is a shouting praise. You don't sing it; you shout it. A shout commands our victory. It stills the enemy. Our praise puts evil to flight.

---

8 "Hebrews & Greek Words for Praise," *Worship Basic 101*, https://sites.google.com/site/worshipbasic101/about-praise--worship/hebrews--greek-words-for-praise.

How do I praise God? With my voice! A shout is spiritual warfare. Psalm 47:1 (AMP) says, "Oh, clap your hands, all you people! Shout to God with the voice of triumph!" The Message translation describes it in a much more exuberant way: "Applause, everyone. Bravo, bravissimo! Shout God-songs at the top of your lungs!" I love the imagery of this! It paints a picture of loud, clamoring, chaotic, noisy, euphoric praise of a people who are so excited about their victorious God that they are shouting songs as loud as they can! It sounds, based on this scripture, that we are commanded to throw over-the-top celebrations of worship and praise!

> *As we shout unto God, we shout at the devil. The power of an anointed shout will bring breakthrough, deliverance, provision, answers to prayer, and manifestations. It will put demons on the run.*

As we shout *unto* God, we shout *at* the devil. The power of an anointed shout will bring breakthrough, deliverance, provision, answers to prayer, and manifestations. It will put demons on the run.

When my kids were little, one of my daughters—who will remain unnamed—got into my makeup. She was sitting on my bathroom floor right in the middle of a sea of eyeshadow, mascara, blush, and lipstick. She had her back to the door, so she didn't see me come in. I knew by the opened blush and lipstick pallets that she was having a good old time applying my makeup anywhere she could. She didn't have any business playing with my stuff, so I decided to teach her a lesson. I quietly snuck up behind her and shouted, "What are you doing? None of that stuff belongs to you! Drop it right now!"

She jumped up, turned around, dropped everything she had been playing with, and with smeared red lipstick, blue eyeshadow, and pink blush all over her cute little face, ran out the door. Clearly, I would never compare any of my children to the devil—although there are times they've acted like him—the enemy is the same way! He takes off running when you take authority over him. He will flee if you will resist him. Another word for resist is battle. When you battle the enemy, he will leave you alone.

James 4:7 (MSG) says, "Yell a loud no to the Devil and watch him make himself scarce." This is how you will win against whatever is coming against you. Why? Because shouting is spiritual warfare. Shouting is a battle cry. It's a cry of victory. The enemy, who has been defeated, is no match for you when you give God praise! When you shout, it stirs up your faith, and God releases His power. It is a powerful weapon against the devil.

Psalm 8:2 (AMPC) says, "Out of the mouths of babes and unweaned infants You have established strength because of Your foes, that You might silence the enemy and the avenger." In other words, Jesus is the big brother who stands behind you when the bully on the playground is pestering you. You may have to *face* the bully, but you'll never have to *fight* the bully. You have a big brother who will silence the voice of your enemy.

I have a greater understanding today of the power of praise than I did when I first wrote "Shout." I have a greater revelation of spiritual warfare and how to defeat the enemy. The truth

Scan to download the song from this chapter.

is that he's already defeated, but you and I have to learn to defeat the fear, doubt, worry, inadequacy, self-limitations, and every other issue the enemy tricks us into believing, so we can walk in the authority Jesus died for us to have.

PRAYER

Thank You, Jesus, for the authority I have in Your name. I will no longer allow the enemy to intimidate and harass me with fear and doubt. I will step out in faith and obey what You have called me to do. I will not put my trust in my own ability—instead, I put my faith in You. Because of the cross, the enemy has been conquered and is under my feet. Today, I will give You a shout of praise, knowing and believing You have silenced my enemies. In Jesus's name. Amen!

FIFTEEN

THE GREAT EXCHANGE

♪

His joy, my strength
His grace, my peace
My fear erased—my
     heart is free!
His joy, my strength
His grace, my peace
My sin erased—my
     heart is free!
His joy, my strength
His grace, my peace
My fear erased—my
     heart is free!

This is the great exchange
I'm trading my sorrows for
     the garment of praise
Heaven is open every
     time I praise

This is the great, this is
     the great exchange

Beauty for ashes and
     joy for my pain
He turns weeping into dancing
     every time I praise
Burdens are lifting, doubts
     begin to cease
He removes the heavy
     burdens and brings
     the sweetest peace

My fear he is taking
replacing with dancing
And singing a song of
     deliverance
A song of deliverance

MUSIC AND LYRICS BY MARTHA MUNIZZI

"Okay, Martha, we need you to just sing the song. Sing us your song. Go ahead."

"Okay. I will, but I'm not really sure if it's good enough."

"Okay. Well, Martha, we won't know until you sing it."

"I know, but I'm just not sure if it's good."

"Okay. Listen. We're here for you. You've got to stop second-guessing yourself. Come on. You've been saying that all day—about every song you've written. We need you to just be confident and sing the song."

"All right—here it goes . . . . *This is the great exchange. I'm trading my sorrows for the garment of praise. Heaven is open every time I praise. This is the great, this is the great exchange.* What do you think?"

"Are you kidding? I love it. Believe me. We're gonna make that a great song."

That's the voice of my friend Terrence Palmer who was my bass player. He really challenged me and slightly rebuked me to stop second-guessing myself and just hand over what I felt the Lord had given me. I needed to sing the songs out loud so that better musicians around me could take them and make them even better.

"The Great Exchange" has become one of my favorite songs that I've ever written, and it really exemplifies Psalm 30. The psalmist is saying to the Lord, "You've turned my mourning into dancing. You have taken off my sackcloth and clothed me with joy that my soul may sing praise to you and not be silent. Oh, Lord, my God. I will give thanks to you forever!"

That is what happens when we praise God. God turns our mourning into dancing. He takes off our sorrows and puts on our joy. That is so powerful to think about—just as a practice—when we do it every single day. When we worship God, something's being exchanged; something supernatural happens when we get in God's presence. Daily time in God's presence is critical because every day we face battles, difficulties, and trials that bring anxieties, fears, and worry into our lives. Sometimes, they actually become a garment or a cloak that we wear around us. When we come before the Lord, and we bring Him our worries and our fears, He takes them and turns them into joy. He turns them into singing and dancing.

> *When we worship God, something's being exchanged; something supernatural happens when we get in God's presence.*

How powerful is that? That's what you and I have access to. Joy, strength, peace, and everything else we need is found in God's presence. I encourage you to make it your life goal, your daily goal, and your priority to say, "God, I refuse to allow anxiety to weigh me down. I refuse to let sickness, problems, the past, and temptations hinder me. I'm going to jump every day into Your presence and experience this great exchange for myself!"

Scan to download the song from this chapter.

Don't wait any longer. Don't hesitate. Begin to move into God's presence and experience the great exchange.

PRAYER

Thank You, Jesus, for the joy, strength, and peace that You give in exchange for my sorrow, weakness, and fear. I step out in faith today, and exchange my mourning for rejoicing in Your presence. I refuse to let the trials of this life weigh me down. I want to move in Your presence and experience the great exchange for myself. In Jesus's name. Amen.

SIXTEEN

HE'S ALREADY PROVIDED

♪

He's already provided, He's
already provided
Everything you need, He's
already provided

Every promise you can claim
Just ask it in His name
'Cause everything you need
He's already provided

MUSIC AND LYRICS BY MARTHA MUNIZZI

E verything you need in life . . . the Lord has already provided for you. So, whatever you think you need—YOU ALREADY HAVE IT! Second Peter 1:3 (NLT) tells us, "By his divine power, God has given us everything we need for living a godly life." Notice it says HAS GIVEN. That is *past* tense. That means it has already happened. Often, we spend our time praying and asking God for things that He has already provided. Many believers are constantly begging God, trying to convince Him to do something for them, when the truth is He has already done it!

I wrote this when we were in debt—but we had big dreams. I had lots of notes on a piece of paper about how God had provided for us, but all of a sudden, these six words popped out! *He's already provided everything you need.*

One of the names of God is *Jehovah Jireh*. The meaning of that name is "God provides" or "God has seen ahead and made provision." God knows the beginning from the end. He knows everything that is going to happen in your life. He has seen ahead and made provision for your every need. You just need to be where God is directing you in order to be where His provision is.

God HAS blessed you. Ephesians 1:3 (NLT) says, "All praise to God, the Father of our Lord Jesus Christ, who has blessed us with every spiritual blessing. . . ." Again, notice it says God "has blessed." You have already been blessed with every blessing! So, it is really counterproductive to spend time praying and asking God to do something He's already done or waiting for Him to bless you.

If you're in a place of needing God to meet a need instead of asking God to provide, begin by thanking the Lord, according to Philippians 4:19 (NASB 1995) for "supplying all of your needs according to His riches in glory." If you're sick, instead of asking God to heal you, start by thanking the Lord that "by His stripes, I *am* healed" (1 Peter 2:24, NKJV, emphasis added). If you're needing direction for a decision, instead of waiting for God to do something, begin declaring Psalm 37:23 (NKJV): "[My] steps are ordered of the Lord."

The Word of God is filled with promises of what God has provided for us. Second Peter 1:4 (NIV) says that God has given us "great and precious promises. . . ." He has promised healing—and He has already provided it. God has promised prosperity—and it has already been provided. He has promised you joy and peace—and He has already provided them. Whatever you need—YOU HAVE IT! You just need to possess God's promises by faith.

What most believers are missing is knowledge. Too many don't even know what God's Word says. They are not aware that it's filled with the promises of God. Hosea 4:6 (NLT) says, "My people are being destroyed because they have no knowledge." We need to ask, according to Ephesians 1:17, that we would have the Spirit of wisdom and revelation—the knowledge of Jesus and His Word.

> *God has promised healing—and He has already provided it. God has promised prosperity—and it has already been provided. He has promised you joy and peace—and He has already provided them. Whatever you need—YOU HAVE IT! You just need to possess God's promises by faith.*

Begin today by reading, hearing, speaking, and meditating on God's Word. The Bible encourages us to meditate on the Word day and night (Joshua 1:8; Psalms 1:2), to study it (2 Timothy 2:15), and to speak it (2 Corinthians 4:13). Hiding the Word in your heart is the key to obtaining God's promises!

Scan to download the song from this chapter.

PRAYER

Dear Jesus, I cast all my cares on You—all the financial concerns I am currently facing. Lord, I cast every worry over finances down at Your feet. Your Word promises You will supply all my needs according to the riches in Christ. I will stand on Your Word and trust You to provide. I am believing for resources to be available to me at the right time because Your timing is impeccable. I am believing for increase and favor over my finances. I cast all my burdens on You. You are the great provider, and my trust is in You! In Jesus's name. Amen!

SEVENTEEN

GLORIOUS

♪

When you come into
His presence
Lifting up the name of Jesus
And you hear the music playin'
And you see the people praisin'
Just forget about your worries
Let your troubles fall
behind you
Don't you wait another
minute
Just get up and on your
feet and . . .

Get to dancing, singing,
jumping, leaping
Get to shouting, and make it
loud, and make it glorious
Start rejoicing, praising,
lifting, raising
Get to shouting, and
make it loud
And make His praise
glorious, glorious

MUSIC AND LYRICS BY MARTHA MUNIZZI & ISRAEL HOUGHTON

Shout for joy to God, all the earth! Sing the glory of his name; make his praise glorious. Say to God, "How awesome are your deeds! So great is your power that your enemies cringe before you.
—PSALM 66:1-3 (NIV)

I wrote "Glorious" several years ago when I was actually headed to the last rehearsal for the live recording of *The Best Is Yet to Come*. The night before, I could not sleep. It was one o'clock in the morning and getting later, and I had a very early flight to catch the next day to Austin, Texas, where the band and singers were awaiting my arrival. I had the privilege of working with Israel Houghton and Aaron Lindsey—two great producers—and we were about to go to Lakewood Church in Houston, Texas, to record our live album.

This was a huge opportunity. I could not believe God had opened this door for me, and I was so excited. We had most of the songs ready to go, but I knew the record needed one more. I just felt like there was one missing piece. Plus, I'd remembered weeks before—when my sister, Mary, had called me—we were talking, and she said, "Have you ever looked at the scripture 'Make his praise glorious' in Psalm 66?

I said, "Well, sure!"

She replied, "Somebody needs to write a song based on that scripture!"

So this was still on my mind and in my heart when I was struggling to go to sleep, so I said, "God, what is it that you wanna say?"

Still awake, I was so frustrated that I got up and started walking around my kitchen, praying, "God, please give me this song. I know it's there. I know there's something there." And I just began to really press on the Holy Spirit to sing through me. (This was back in the day before we had cell phone apps at our disposal that could record really quickly. I'd actually have to go into another room, pick up a landline phone, and call my house phone so that I could record it on my voicemail. That's how it was back then! Then retrieving it—that was a whole other challenge, but I knew there was something that

God wanted to sing to me and through me.) All of a sudden, as I said, "God, please birth this song, just give me the song," it was as if a gush of creativity began to flow. I began to sing the lyrics to the verses, and the chorus came quickly thereafter. I was stunned. I grabbed my phone, called my voicemail, and left it as a message. Then I was able to go right to sleep.

The next morning, I flew to Austin and walked into where the singers and musicians were. I said, "Hey, guys, I've got one more song. Is it too late?"

They said, "No, let's hear it!"

So I sang it to them, and they loved it.

They said, "This is something different. This is unique."

Right there, we finished the bridge that says, "I was created to make your praise glorious," and recorded it. The night of the recording, after having rehearsed most of the day before, I was completely hoarse. I had no voice left, but somehow God's strength infused me, and I was able to sing with a full voice throughout the whole night. It was really a supernatural miracle. And this song—we call it "Glorious"—has gone global. It has been one of my signature songs—sung in churches and in different languages all over the world—and I am just so blessed to be associated with it.

That word glorious is found in the Old Testament. If you look at the Hebrew definition, it means "heaviness" or "weight."[9] It was used in everyday speech when people expressed the honor or the worth of a person, maybe in the material sense, and then to express the idea of the importance, the greatness, the honor, the splendor, and the power of someone. So this word is not a throwaway word. Glorious is not a

---

9 Strong's Hebrew: 3513. כָּבַד (Kabad or KABED)—to Be Heavy, Weighty, or Burdensome, https://biblehub.com/hebrew/3513.htm.

light word. It's a heavy word. It's a weighty word. And it's important for us to know that when we make God's praise glorious, when we tell our problems how big our God is, we're really telling the world how great our God is. When we look at our obstacles and say, "You're not a problem for God," then when we share that with someone else, we're telling the world how great our God is. Then God begins to work behind the scenes on our behalf!

> *Cringe—I love that word because your praise causes the enemy to cringe or recoil and shrink back in pain. Your praise causes the devil pain. I love the thought of that because we often allow the enemy to cause us to recoil, shrink back, back down, or cower in fear.*

When you declare God's power over your life, the Bible says that the enemy will cringe. Cringe—I love that word because your praise causes the enemy to cringe or recoil and shrink back in pain. Your praise causes the devil pain. I love the thought of that! Instead of allowing the enemy to cause us to recoil, shrink-back, back-down, or cower in fear, we need to remind ourselves how awesome our God is and make the enemy cringe instead! When you shout for joy, when you take the time every day to make God's praise glorious, that's what's happening in the spirit realm. The enemy is cringing. I love that. That's the weight of it—the power of it. That's what happens when you and I make God's praise glorious.

Scan to download the song from this chapter.

So take time today to pray, but not just pray, but declare God's power over your life, and watch the enemy recoil and shrink back in pain. Watch the enemy cringe.

PRAYER

Lord, today I shake off heaviness, and I put on a garment of praise. I love You, and I love being in Your presence. I want to be a person who keeps my eyes on You and makes Your praise glorious, no matter what I am going through or how difficult my situation might be. You are worthy of my best and highest praise, and I will give You the praise of which You are worthy. In Jesus's name. Amen.

EIGHTEEN

MY STRENGTH

♪

My strength, my strength
O the joy of the Lord is
My strength, my strength
O the joy of the Lord is

My strength—that is enough
To overcome the world

You're the joy no one
    can take away
You're the joy no one
    can take away

You're the peace inside
    I can't explain
You're the strength I need—
    You will always be

Stronger, stronger
I'm getting stronger
The joy of the Lord
It makes me stronger
Greater, greater
My God is greater
His power, His power
It makes me stronger

MUSIC AND LYRICS BY MARTHA MUNIZZI, ISRAEL HOUGHTON, DANIELLE MUNIZZI

But the fruit of the Spirit is love, joy, peace, patience,
kindness, goodness, faithfulness, gentleness,
self-control; against such things there is no law.
—GALATIANS 5:22-23 (ESV)

E very day, we face challenging circumstances and difficult decisions. We have a choice to respond by faith, or we can let fear
dictate our decision-making. The response we choose determines the
type of seed we sow—fear or faith. The seed we sow determines the
fruit we produce, and the fruit we produce determines the type of
person we are becoming. When we react in our own strength, we plant
unhealthy seeds that produce fruits of the sinful nature: bitterness,
worry, frustration, harshness, evil, dishonesty, violence, and indul-
gence. These choices prevent us from becoming the person God has
created us to be and stunt our growth in our relationship with him.

> *When we trust God, we plant seeds that*
> *open our hearts to be filled with the fruit*
> *of the Spirit: love, joy, peace, patience,*
> *kindness, goodness, faithfulness, gentleness,*
> *and self-control. We reflect the image*
> *of Christ to the world and experience*
> *the very nature of God in our lives.*

When we trust God, we plant seeds that open our hearts to be
filled with the fruit of the Spirit: love, joy, peace, patience, kindness,
goodness, faithfulness, gentleness, and self-control. We reflect the
image of Christ to the world and experience the very nature of God
in our lives. We don't have the power to produce this good fruit on
our own, but we do have the choice to plant good seeds. Fear or faith!

If you focus on developing fruit, you won't have to worry about
breaking any of God's commandments. That's what He meant in Gala-
tions by "there is no law." You can either focus on rules or character.

If you focus on rules, you might break one. If you focus on character, it's harder for you to break rules.

What happens a lot of times is that we dwell on our problems and don't take advantage of what already belongs to us. That's why we need to put spiritual things first. All you need to do to grow in love is abide in Him and let Him abide in you through prayer, the Word, and communion with Him. Then, exercise the love that you have on the inside. It may take time for the fruit of love to mature. We may not see the full-grown, mature fruit for a while, but at least we can see some buds starting to appear, and we can know our love is growing and developing.

The Greek word for joy is *chara*, which is where we get the word character from. Joy is not happiness. Happiness is more temporary as it is a result of short-term contentment. Joy is deeper. It's not dependent on circumstances. It doesn't come and go; it remains. I experienced a dark season after my parents divorced. The spirit of heaviness was on me, and I couldn't shake it off. If you struggle with the spirit of heaviness, it helps to understand the underlying cause first. Once you know this, you will understand why the methods to lift it work. A psychiatrist once said that people who struggle with neurotic disorders, such as depression or anxiety, almost always have a habit of fault-finding. Either they focus on faults within themselves or faults with other people. No matter what is good in their lives, they concentrate on what is wrong or lacking. When I used to suffer from bouts of depression years ago, I was like that, but then I discovered God's promise about why Jesus came in Isaiah 61:3 (NKJV):

"To console those who mourn in Zion, To give them beauty for ashes,
The oil of joy for mourning, The garment of praise for the spirit

of heaviness; That they may be called trees of righteousness, The planting of the Lord, that He may be glorified."

Joy comes when we live in God's presence. It took me years to understand what Nehemiah 8:10 (NKJV), "The joy of the Lord is [my] strength" means. I always interpreted it to be talking about the joy that God puts inside me, the fruit of the Spirit, or the joy I have. However, this is not what God says here. He says the joy OF the Lord, the joy that God has—not the joy we get from God—is our strength.

Jesus said in John 15:11 (NIV), "I have told you this so that my joy may be in you and that your joy may be complete."

In the book of Nehemiah, Nehemiah and his people had been ravaged by war. They'd had to mortgage their fields, their vineyards, and homes to get grain during the famine. They'd borrowed money to pay the king's tax and subjected their children to slavery, and they were powerless to redeem them because their fields and vineyards belonged to other people. But what did Nehemiah instruct the Israelites to do?

"Go home and prepare a feast, holiday food and drink; and share it with those who don't have anything: This day is holy to God. Don't feel bad. The joy of God is your strength!" —Nehemiah 8:10 (MSG)

Joy is not an emotion that can be forced, fabricated, or faked.

Joy comes when we feel secure in the Lord.

Joy comes when we have clear direction for our life.

What is my strength? It is knowing how loved I am by Him and how much He wants to have a relationship with me. Nothing you do will make God love you more. He is happy when you recognize His love for you! Get excited about God's love for you! Hebrews 12:2 (NIV), "For the joy that was set before him he endured the cross," reveals the only reason Jesus endured the cross. It was because of the joy of reconciliation with you! The joy of having—once again—an unbroken relationship with you. The joy of unbroken fellowship with you. He has found His pearl of great price, and your value in

Scan to download the song from this chapter.

His eyes made Him able to endure anything, even the cross, in order to have you close to Him.

Jesus said in Luke 15:7 (ESV), "I tell you that in the same way, there will be more *joy* in heaven over one sinner who repents than over ninety-nine righteous persons who need no repentance" (emphasis added). Our strength comes from the revelation of who He is, how He feels towards us, and what He loves. It is rejoicing IN Him that will bring us strength.

From personal experience, I know that if I go through hard times, I can still rejoice in Him—in who He is, what He loves, and how He feels about me. If I turn my eyes away from my problems in hard times and rejoice in Him—in who He is—then I gain strength to face whatever life throws at me. True joy is the result of a right relationship with God.

PRAYER

Lord Jesus, I need to be in right relationship with You to experience real joy. Today, I commit everything to You: my plans, my will, and my way of doing things. I am so thankful for the love You have for me; because You love me, I can overcome every hardship I face. I rebuke depression and pull down every negative thought that challenges Your truth. I am confident and secure in who You are, and Your joy is the only strength I need. In Jesus's name. Amen!

NINETEEN

NO CONDEMNATION

♪

There is no condemnation
For those in Christ Jesus
By His blood, I have
    been made free
There is no condemnation
For those in Christ Jesus
By His blood, I have
    been redeemed

Because of His forgiveness
I don't have to live with
    shame anymore
Because of His redemption
No more condemnation—
    there's no more

There's no more
There's no more guilt
There's no more shame
There's no more

Christ who died
Raised to life
Made a way for me
There's no depth
There's no height
That can separate me
From His love

MUSIC AND LYRICS BY MARTHA MUNIZZI, DANIELLE MUNIZZI, ANTHONY EVANS

"Therefore, [there is] now no condemnation (no adjudging guilty of wrong) for those who are in Christ Jesus, who live [and] walk not after the dictates of the flesh, but after the dictates of the Spirit.

For the law of the Spirit of life [which is] in Christ Jesus [the law
of our new being] has freed me from the law of sin and of death."
—ROMANS 8:1-2 (AMPC)

For two years during the COVID-19 pandemic, we all wore masks everywhere we went to try and prevent the spreading of a virus that had invaded our world. Wearing a mask, at first, wasn't easy to get used to. In the beginning, I would forget to bring a mask with me and invariably have to take that long walk back to my car to get it every time I stopped at the grocery store. It took a while for me to adapt to mask-wearing, but before long, I made sure to put masks in every nook and cranny of my car, so I wouldn't forget to wear one.

Although I resented wearing a mask at first, I soon began to enjoy the benefits of wearing one. I could go out with no makeup on. I could just throw a hat on, cover most of my face, and hide. I was able to hide behind a mask—hide my identity—and before long, I liked the ease of this newfound way of life.

Can you relate to that?

> *If you are not careful, it can become easy*
> *to hide behind a mask of self-preservation,*
> *fear, and insecurity that will keep you from*
> *being all that God made you to be. Fear*
> *and self-preservation will keep you from*
> *discovering who God made you to be and*
> *from experiencing real freedom in Christ.*

If you are not careful, it can become easy to hide behind a mask of self-preservation, fear, and insecurity that will keep you from being all that God made you to be. Fear and self-preservation will keep you from discovering who God made you to be and from experiencing real freedom in Christ. Masks of insecurity cultivate imposter syndrome and causes you to create a false identity of who you are.

One time, when I was singing at a conference, I ran into a young man backstage carrying a case of bottled water and wearing a conference badge with his name—Samuel—on it. He was friendly and helpful. When he saw that the musicians and I needed to get ready, he offered to show us where in the green room to put our belongings: bags, purses, valuables, etc. I hid my purse with my wallet and a new pair of sunglasses (an expensive gift which had been given to me) behind a couch. Promising us that everything would be safe, he locked the room.

After I finished singing, and we went to the merch table, I noticed that our boxes of CDs were already open. I thought it was strange, but I didn't think much of it. I went ahead and signed my CDs and took photos with attendees. It wasn't long before we packed up, retrieved our stuff from the green room, and got in the car to go to the hotel. Upon checking my purse, I noticed my cash was gone. I was only a little worried until I realized my glasses were gone too! It was then that I knew I had been robbed! After telling our driver, I immediately went into detective mode.

My first thought was of the kid I had run into who was carrying the water. His name, Samuel, popped back into my head, so I reported him to the woman in charge of the event. Although she said they didn't have anyone by that name working on the event, it didn't take her long to realize who he was, and she called his mother. He wasn't home yet, so we created a sting operation. His mom said she would be quiet about it and look in his backpack when he walked in the door. Not surprised, she found all of my stuff and drove him to our hotel to personally return it. The mother was crying. Samuel was embarrassed as he put all of my stolen items in front of me on the desk in the lobby of the hotel room and sank back in a chair with his head down.

I went into Momma mode. I asked him why he had pretended to be something he wasn't. I found out later he had been telling people he was an executive for a record label! "Why," I said, "don't you stop pretending to be someone you're not and actually work to become a record label executive? Go to school and become the authentic person you are pretending to be!" I prayed that he would be the worst thief who ever lived and that every time he stole, he would get caught and not get away with anything. Instead of pressing charges I prayed with him that God would get a hold of his heart and that he would recognize his gifts, start living authentically, and make his momma proud!

That story is extreme, but it's true! How many of us are pretending in order to impress someone or are hiding behind fear and inadequacy, afraid to be vulnerable, worried that if someone found out who we really are, we would be exposed? As a result, we run, and we hide. It's called imposter syndrome, and it's the experience of feeling like a phony—as though at any moment you are going to be found out as a fraud—like you don't belong where you are, and you only got there by chance.

Shame and condemnation cause us to wear masks to hide our identity. Masks cover us. Masks hide us from the world, from the people around us. We don't have to be fully seen. You can paint anything you want on a mask, but it's not real. When we wear masks, we carve a piece of ourselves out—withholding parts of ourselves as unworthy. But in relationships, we can't be truly healed unless we offer up all the pieces to God. It's like handing someone a broken vase and asking him or her to fix it but holding back two or three of the broken pieces.

I heard a pastor from Hope City Church in Indianapolis, Indiana, say, "Masks make shallow what God has intended to be deep. Everything in our lives get[s] cheated when we choose to hide behind our masks." Take off the mask of fear; stop running and hiding from the things in your life that are oppressing you.

You will never know the healing power of grace until you take off your mask(s). Grace must be allowed to enter in, and if you are pretending, hiding, or putting on a false identity, you can't allow grace to do the work of healing you, so you can discover your true identity.

Whether it's a mask of insecurity, fear, inadequacy, or failure, take it off, and lean into who God has created you to be! God does not define your life based on what you have done or who you are. He defines your life based on what Jesus has done for you and who Jesus is in you. And that's the only thing that matters.

Romans 8:1 (NIV) says, "Therefore, there is now no condemnation for those who are in Christ Jesus." There is no condemnation—none whatsoever—for the believer in Jesus Christ. Paul is not saying there is now no *cause* for condemnation. That wouldn't be true. You and I fail, we stumble and we fall, and we veer from the path. If God were to look down from heaven and judge you moment by moment, He'd find plenty of cause for condemnation in you. So that's not what Paul's saying. Is he saying, "There is, therefore now, no failure for those who are in Christ Jesus?" No. He's not saying you won't stumble or struggle. He is saying there is no condemnation, no judgment, and no punishment for those who are following Christ. You will stumble, you may fall, you may trip and make a thousand mistakes, you may sin and get off the path, but for the believer, you are not condemned.

Again, Paul said in Romans 8:1 (ESV), "There is therefore now *no* condemnation for those who are in Christ"

Scan to download the song from this chapter.

(emphasis added). The key is to stay IN Christ! Stay free from sin which causes shame and guilt. Take off the masks that keep you from walking in total freedom. You can because on the cross, Jesus took our shame and guilt onto Himself and died in our place. He took the punishment we deserved. He took back the keys of death, hell, and the grave and gave us the power over sin. Now we no longer follow after the flesh or give in to our sin nature. We follow the voice of the Holy Spirit, and we are led by the desires of the Spirit. What a beautiful way to live—free from sin, free from shame, free from any and all condemnation. All sins are forgiven! There is no condemnation for your past mistakes, so walk in that freedom!

PRAYER

Father, in the name of Jesus, I thank You that there is no condemnation for those who are in Christ. I have been liberated by the blood of Jesus, and sin has no power over me. I will be everything You have called me to be, and I will walk in freedom!

TWENTY

YOU'VE BEEN SO GOOD

♪

You've been so good
And I really wanna
   thank You, Jesus
You've been so good
And I really wanna
   thank you, Lord
You've been so good
And I really wanna
   thank You, Jesus
I really wanna thank You
I really wanna thank
   You, Lord

You made a way where
   there was no way
You gave me joy down in
   my heart to stay
You changed my life, and I
   never will be the same
And now I've got to lift
   my voice and say
You've been so good!

MUSIC AND LYRICS BY MARTHA MUNIZZI

D an and I were just getting started in our music career and had recently released our *The Best Is Yet to Come* album. Things were going well, and the album was selling, as we liked to say, "out of the trunk of our car," when, to our surprise, major label executives started reaching out to us about signing us to a recording contract. At the time, we thought if we were going to have real success with an album, we would have to sign with a major record label. Every successful recording artist we had known up to that point had signed with labels, so we figured it was the only option for us.

Over the following weeks, Dan and I met with several label executives who all wanted to sign me, but we had a hard time agreeing to their terms. Most of them wanted us to sign contracts that would give them ownership of our copyrights which meant that they would own my songs. We didn't feel right about it, but that's how the industry worked at that time, so we were confused about what we should do. We needed advice but didn't know whom to turn to. We kept asking the Lord for wisdom and trusted that He would lead us to someone who might be able to give us the advice we needed before we signed with a label.

One day, my husband told me that Donnie McClurkin was hosting a conference in Orlando, Florida, where we live. I was excited until I found out it would be held on Thanksgiving weekend. I really wanted to attend the conference, but I did not want to miss spending time with my family. I didn't get to see them very often, and Thanksgiving is our sacred tradition. It's a very special time for my mother, my sisters, and all of our children to be together, and there was no way I was going to cut the celebration short. I told Dan that even though I would love to go, there was no way we could miss out on Thanksgiving with my family.

A few days before the conference, Dan couldn't wait to tell me of the latest development with the conference. He said that he had heard from Donnie's manager and found out that because we were local, if we wanted to, we could be guests at the conference. This could be a huge open door for us! I was still feeling conflicted, but I was becoming more open to the idea that our Thanksgiving holiday might look a little different. Honestly, I had already started to sense that we were supposed to be at the conference whether I sang or not. It was becoming more apparent that there was a bigger reason we needed to be there, so I happily agreed to go.

On Thanksgiving day, as soon as we had finished eating lunch, my husband looked at me and said, "Are you ready to go? We have to be there for sound check very soon." My sisters are both in the ministry, so they understood and completely encouraged me to cut Thanksgiving day with them short and go to the conference. To be honest, I was a little disappointed that I would miss out on eating the leftovers that are always the best part of Thanksgiving, but I could eat a reheated turkey sandwich any day of the week. My entire family felt that this was an opportunity I could not afford to miss out on.

Dan and I excitedly packed up our CDs and other merchandise in our car, and as we headed to the conference center, I said, "I still can't believe Donnie invited me to his conference. I didn't think he would even know who I am!"

Dan's response was not the response I anticipated. He said, "Well, technically, we weren't invited. We invited ourselves. When I heard that Donnie was coming to Orlando for his conference, I reached out to his manager and let them know that we live here in Orlando, and if they needed our help in any way, we were available. When his manager asked if you would be available to sing, I told him yes. I told him we didn't need any money or anything. They could just allow us to be a part, set up a table, and sell our product. Aren't you excited?"

I couldn't believe it. I was stunned! "This whole time, I thought that we had been invited, and now I'm finding out that we invited ourselves? How could you not tell me this? I had no idea you asked if we could come! This is so embarrassing!"

Dan stopped me and said, "Listen, Martha. God has given you a lot of great worship songs, and this is an opportunity to promote your ministry. We have to make ourselves available whenever there is an open door."

I knew he was right, but I was still upset. Now I didn't know what to expect when we got to the conference. Would anyone even care that we were there?

As we drove, the Holy Spirit started talking to me about my attitude. Once again, God was testing my motives to make sure I was ready for what He had in store for me. I had no idea that the path God had planned for me was going to have a lot of twists and turns and that there were going to be more disappointments and surprises in my future. This was just part of the journey, so I had to humble myself and not be preoccupied with my own desire to be seen. By the time we got to the venue, my attitude had already started to change. I really was excited about being there and hoping for the chance to be with Donnie McClurkin and experience the conference.

I walked into this large, open room and could see all of the musicians and singers onstage getting a sound check for the evening service. Donnie McClurkin was standing onstage with his back to us, and as he turned around and saw me, he said, "Is that Martha Munizzi? I am so glad you're here!"

I had no idea Donnie McClurkin even knew who I was. AND he pronounced my name right!

Then Donnie said, "Martha, come onstage, and sing your song "God is Here," and my singers and I will back you up." I could not believe that in a moment's time, I had gone from standing in the back of the room—not knowing what to expect—to singing onstage with Donnie McClurkin and his family singing backup for me! Donnie asked me to sing during the opening night of the conference, and I said absolutely yes!

At the conference, Dan and I got a chance to spend time with Donnie's manager, Roger Holmes. At the beginning of this chapter, I wrote how Dan and I had been praying for God to lead us to someone who could advise us on what label we should sign with. We desperately needed advice on what to do about the label contracts that we'd been given and someone to lead us in the right direction.

After a few minutes of explaining our situation to Roger, he said, "If I were you, I would sign with a distribution company and stay independent as long as you can. You're already doing well on your own, so why don't you just stay an independent artist, and become your own label?"

We had never even considered that idea!

Roger gave us the best advice we'd ever received, and from that moment on, we decided to become independent artists. We've learned years later that we set the standard for many new artists coming up behind us in the industry. We helped shape the entire industry, with many artists becoming independent.

If you will follow the voice of the Holy Spirit and be willing to sacrifice your own comfort, God will synchronize your steps with the right people at the right time. Now, I look back on the time I cried over leaving my family on Thanksgiving and realize that God had such a bigger plan for me—a divine appointment scheduled that set us up for success for years to come!

The Holy Spirit knows things you don't know. He knows what your purpose is, and He wants to connect you. He knew where I needed to be on that Thanksgiving day all those years ago.

We need a daily ongoing relationship with God, so we can know exactly what He wants us to do right now.

Scan to download the song from this chapter.

There are all kinds of voices trying to influence us every day. But what makes you a great man, woman, leader, parent, or person is being able to shut out the outside voices and hear what the Spirit of the Lord is saying!

Once you know the purpose that God has for your life, you need to start speaking your purpose every day! It's one thing to know it, but it's a whole other level when you speak it! When you line up your speech with what you know, you bring yourself into alignment with God's purpose for your life. The enemy can try, but he won't be able to pull you into confusion or chaos because now you have clear direction!

PRAYER

Father, my desire is to have a daily, ongoing relationship with You, so I can know exactly what You want me to do. Help me shut out all the voices that try to influence me and help me hear what Your Spirit is saying to me every day.

You are so good, and I am so grateful! I am convinced You have a clear purpose for my life, and I thank You for giving me the wisdom to know and walk in that purpose. I will not only believe that I have a purpose but also align myself with Your will and speak it over my life every day until I see it come to pass. I will line up my actions and words with Your will and not allow the enemy to pull me into confusion or chaos. Lord, You have been good to me, and I will continue to put my trust in You! In Jesus's name. Amen.

TWENTY-ONE

ASK

Ask and it will be given to you
Seek and you will find
Knock and the door will
  be open to you
Just ask, Just ask

We ask for our healing
We ask for salvation
We ask for our breakthrough

We ask for the nations
We ask for Your power
We ask for Your presence
We ask!

Exceedingly, abundantly
Far above all we
Could ask or think

MUSIC AND LYRICS BY MARTHA MUNIZZI, DANIELLE MUNIZZI, ANTHONY EVANS

I love using scripture to write songs. You won't find more powerful words to sing about! God's Word is so full of life and hope, and when put it to melody, it will live in your heart forever.

Our daughter, Danielle, and I had the privilege of writing "Ask" with our good friend Anthony Evans. This song practically wrote itself as it was written in about fifteen minutes over the phone. We all loved the verses found in Matthew 7 and wanted to write a song about the power of asking God in order to receive His promises. Jesus said:

"Ask and it will be given to you; seek and you will find; knock and the door will be opened to you. For everyone who asks receives; the one who seeks finds; and to the one who knocks, the door will be opened."
—Matthew 7:7-8 (NIV)

This is a beautiful translation, but it suggests a single request will get the job done. It's true; sometimes, a single request is enough. You ask Him. You thank Him for it. And you keep praising Him until you see the prayer answered. Other times, it takes persistent faith to receive God's promises. You have to go after it with determination that won't quit. That's why I like how the Amplified Bible translates Matthew 7:7-8:

Keep on asking and it will be given you; keep on seeking and you will find; keep on knocking [reverently] and [the door] will be opened to you. For everyone who keeps on asking receives; and he who keeps on seeking finds; and to him who keeps on knocking, [the door] will be opened.

This is a promise from God. So long as what you desire is His will—and His Word is His will—you can be assured that if you keep on asking, keep on seeking, and keep on knocking, you will eventually receive the promise. "Therefore, I tell you; whatever you ask for in prayer, believe that you have received it, and it will be yours." (Mark 11:24, NIV)

So long as what you desire is His will—and His Word is His will—you can be assured that if you keep on asking, keep on seeking, and keep on knocking, you will eventually receive the promise.

ASK

Jesus said in Luke 11:19 (NKJV), "So I say to you, ask, and it will be given to you; seek, and you will find; knock, and it will be opened to you." He gave us three very simple commands: ask, seek, and knock. You'll notice they form an acronym: ASK—Ask, Seek, and Knock. Each one of these is a command; cumulatively, they are steps that teach us how to pray. God wants to work in your life to transform the way you talk to him.

First of all, Jesus commands us to ask. To ask means to come to the Lord with your request and with expectancy, knowing that He is your Heavenly Father. He loves you, He hears you, and He cares about you. Jesus said, "I say to you, ask, and it will be given to you." You don't have to know King James English to pray. You don't have to have a specialized vocabulary to pray. You don't even have to know all that much to pray. All you have to know is that you have a relationship with God through His Son, Jesus Christ, that you've been saved, that God is your Father, that you are His child, and that you are coming to Him, asking, and asking with expectancy.

As Luke 11:11-13 (author paraphrase) goes on, Jesus talked more about asking:

"If a son asks for bread from any father among you, will he give him a stone? Or if he asks for a fish, will he give him a serpent instead of a fish? Or if he asks for an egg, will he offer him a scorpion? If you then, being evil, know how to give good gifts to your children, how much more will your heavenly Father give the Holy Spirit to those who ask Him!"

You come to God asking; He hears, and He answers. God's answer might often sound like no when it's taking a long time to see your prayer answered, but God doesn't really say no to us. More often, He says, "Not yet," or, "I have something so much better."

Jesus started Matthew 7:11 (ESV) by saying, "If you then, being evil, know how to give good gifts to your children"—and by the way, all of us, compared to God and His holiness and His goodness are evil. If we know how to give good gifts to our children, "how much more will your heavenly Father give good gifts to those who ask him" (NLT).

Can I just challenge you in your prayer life? Learn to ask—just come to the Lord and ask. May I also tell you this? Don't be afraid to ask big. Is there anything too big for you to ask God? Sometimes, we miss God's best for our lives because we haven't learned how to ask big.

When you ask, make your requests known to God without fear or reservation. We might not feel confident asking God to move on our behalf because we think we don't deserve it. We don't! He still tells us to ask! Sometimes we don't ask because we don't think God will say yes. But remember: if what you are asking for is in alignment with His will, His answer is already yes!

And don't just ask. The way you approach God is critical. Ask with thanksgiving! When my kids were younger they knew they would always get more from me if they asked me for what they wanted without complaining. Learn how to ask! Just like you want people to approach you when they need something from you, God deserves to be approached with honor and gratefulness. The Bible says, "With thanksgiving, let your requests be made known to God" (Philippians 4:16, ESV). Don't pray worried. Ask in faith! Ask boldly!

SEEK

Not only does the Bible tell us to ask, but the Word of God also tells us to seek. If asking is praying with expectancy, seeking means praying with effort. Notice again what Jesus says in Luke 11:9 (NIV). He says, "Seek, and you will find." Seek—search for something, hunt for something, look for something, and pursue it until you find it. Seeking involves coming before the Lord with a simple question: "Lord, what can I do to be part of Your answer to my prayer?" Some of you just need to write that down because you are missing it at that point. You've been asking, but you haven't been seeking. Seek, and say, "Lord, what can I do to be part of Your answer to my prayer?"

When God created you, He put nearly half of the bones in your body in your hands and in your feet! God made us to act, to do, to seek, and to find. When we pray, we pray with effort—not halfheartedly. Seek is the same word that Jesus uses in Matthew 6:33 (author paraphrase) when He says, "Seek first the kingdom of God, and all these things will be added to you." Seeking means coming to the Lord as you pray and saying, "Lord, what can I do to be part of Your answer to my prayer? Lord, I want my heart to be surrendered to You, and I want my life to be obedient to You so that You can do in me what You want to do." Don't just ask; make sure you seek.

I like to shop, and I love a good sale! Recently, I had my eye on a pair of shoes online I really wanted, but they were too expensive and very hard to find in the stores. I had a link open on my computer with a picture of those shoes, and every once in a while, I would check to see if the shoes had gone on sale. Every time I checked, they became less available, and I was afraid I would miss out on buying a pair if I waited too much longer. One day I walked into a store I had not been in for a long time, and to my surprise, I found the exact same shoes sitting on the rack. And they were on sale! I could not believe it!! I quickly looked for someone who worked there to help me find my size. A few minutes after checking the storage area, I was told that they were out of my size and totally sold out online. I was so disappointed. How could it be that I came so close to getting the shoes I wanted at a discounted price and missed out?

I don't know why, but something in me didn't want to take her word as my final answer. I decided to go on a search throughout the store and look under and over every rack to see if maybe my shoes got placed somewhere by mistake. Anything is possible! I searched inside every box, under every rack, behind the counter, and everywhere else I could think of and came up with nothing. I was about to accept defeat when one of the workers came out of the back of the store and said, "I found one last pair!" They were in the wrong box, but they are the right size!" I'm so glad I didn't take her original response as my final answer. I kept looking with expectation until I found what I wanted.

Of course, things don't always work out like this, but there is a principle here that I believe is important when you pray. Learn to listen, obey the promptings of the Holy Spirit, and keep seeking until He leads you to your promise!

Learn to listen, obey the promptings of the Holy Spirit, and keep seeking until He leads you to your promise!

KNOCK

Some doors are open, but others are locked. Some of the greatest treasures are found behind locked doors. No one locks a house if there's nothing valuable inside. As a matter of fact, the things of greatest value have twenty-four-hour security systems arming them and guard dogs roaming the grounds. You need to learn to knock on some closed doors. Don't think that everything will *Scan to download the song from this chapter.*

happen just because you really want it. The greatest breakthroughs come because we are unafraid to go beyond the ask and seek. We knock on closed doors.

Ask: That's praying with expectancy.

Seek: That's praying with effort. "Lord, what do You want me to do so that I can be a part of Your answer to my prayer?"

Knock: That means praying continuously. Keep on praying; don't give up. Jesus promises an answer. Look with me again at Luke 11:10 (NKJV). The Lord Jesus says, "For everyone who asks receives, and he who seeks finds, and to him who knocks it will be opened." Jesus promises to answer when we pray.

There are a lot of reasons that God tarries in answering a prayer. Sometimes, He's teaching us to appreciate the answer more. Sometimes, He is changing our prayer so that our heart lines up with His heart. Sometimes, He is seeing if we will obey Him and trust Him as we pray. But every time you pray, God is teaching you how to hold on to His hand and to walk through your life with Him. Ask, Seek, and Knock!

PRAYER

Father, Your Word tells me to ask, seek, and knock. Give me the courage to ask and the commitment to keep asking. My prayer today is, "Lord, what can I do to be part of Your answer to my prayer? Lord, I want my heart to be surrendered to You, and I want my life to be obedient to You, so You can do in me what You want to do." I will not be afraid to ask for the greater promises You have for me. You are a good Father who gives good gifts to His children, and I believe You will fulfill every promise I am believing for and expecting in Jesus's name! Amen!

TWENTY-TWO

COME, HOLY SPIRIT, COME

♪

Come, Holy Spirit, Come
Come, Holy Spirit, Come
And abide within us

Rest upon us
Come, Holy Spirit, Come

MUSIC AND LYRICS BY MARTHA MUNIZZI

A few years ago, I was invited to minister at a Benny Hinn crusade. My family has known Pastor Benny and the Hinn family most of our lives and has been impacted and blessed by his ministry. After the crusade, we were ushered into the greenroom where we saw the Who's Who of pastors and ministers from all over the world, sitting and chatting with each other.

We walked over to where Benny was sitting at a tall table with another pastor, excitedly discussing how incredible the crusade was. Mid-sentence, Benny remarked how powerful the Holy Spirit's presence was in the room when he saw my husband, Dan, and me standing beside him. He turned to us and said, "What a powerful anointing there is on your voice. You are remarkable, and God is going to use you all over the world!" I don't remember much after that. All

I remember is feeling heat flow through me, and I knew the presence of God was on me. In one second, I went from standing on both feet, talking to Benny, to falling onto the floor overcome by the power of the Holy Spirit.

Now, there have been a few times that I have experienced being "slain in the Spirit": on the last night of youth camp as a teenager or in a camp-meeting service during a revival. Those moments were powerful, but this was different. I was so overcome with emotion that I could barely get back up without Dan helping me! When I finally was able to stand, I sat down at another table, stunned at what had just happened. I love God's presence, and I am open to receiving anything and everything God desires to do, but "falling out" is not something I would ever just do on my own.

It has to be real, or I am not participating. Do you know what I mean? I've had so-called evangelists pray over me and try to knock me down over the years, and I refused to do a "courtesy drop" just to validate them. If they ever tried, I planted one leg behind me and locked in, so no matter how hard they pushed, they couldn't get me to fall out. I spent a good part of my younger years making fun of people who "fell out" for the fun of it, and I've seen people get sued when someone hit their head on the pew on the way down. (If you're a preacher's kid, you know.) So there was no way I would ever fall unless it was the tangible presence of God! Disclaimer: I also believe that there are times we need to lay prostrate before the Lord, but there is a difference between humbling yourself and being pushed down by someone.

That moment on the floor impacted my life in a powerful way. It's hard to explain unless it's happened to you, but I knew I'd had an encounter with the Holy Spirit. I knew the Holy Spirit was in the room. Since then, I've learned so much about who the Holy Spirit is.

The Holy Spirit doesn't need our help. He is our Helper. Jesus said in John 14:16 (CSB), "I will ask the father, and he will give you another counselor to be with you forever." The Greek word for counselor is *parakletos* which describes someone "from close-beside," or "called to one's aid."[10] This means you pick up one side of the wall, and the Holy Spirit will pick up the other side of the wall to help you. This particular translation uses the word counselor; some translations use the word helper, friend, or advocate. He is someone you can relate to regularly.

Let's talk about who the Holy Spirit is: He is our inner voice, and the Holy Spirit has access to all the wisdom and knowledge of God. When we abide in Him, He leads us continually into truth—causing us to grow and mature spiritually. He is our teacher (1 John 2:27), and those who depend on Him will know where to go and what to do because they are following His heavenly directions. Romans 8:14 (NASB) tells us: "For all who are being led by the Spirit of God, these are sons and daughters of God." If you are a child of God, you have access to the guidance of the Holy Spirit.

He is the best guide ever because He has all the information you need from the past, the present, and the future. I am old enough to remember when people did not have GPS software on their phones (or on anything else!). We actually had to keep maps in the glove boxes of our cars—folded maps . . . made of paper! We'd use them to figure out how to get to a new address. Looking back on those old days of studying maps (and asking for directions at gas stations), I wonder how any of us found our destinations. The Holy Spirit is

10 Strong's Greek: 3875. Παράκλητος (Paraklétos)—Called to One's Aid, https://biblehub.com/greek/3875.htm.

like your internal GPS, except that He never gets confused or offers wrong information.

> We need to be developing our ability and our sensitivity to hearing God's voice. The devil condemns; the Holy Spirit convicts. He is the inner voice that you can become familiar with. The devil tells you you're scum. The Holy Spirit reminds you gently, I wouldn't do that if I were you.

If you want to have the Holy Spirit's guidance, you must learn to discern His voice. God speaks in several different ways. He speaks to us through His Word, His presence, pastors, leaders, and authorities, and through dreams and visions. We need to be developing our ability and our sensitivity to hear God's voice. The devil condemns; the Holy Spirit convicts. He is the inner voice that you can become familiar with. The devil tells you you're scum. The Holy Spirit reminds you gently, *I wouldn't do that if I were you.*

The Holy Spirit is your teacher. He will show you what to do, and He will give you power to do it! John 14:26 (NIV) says, "But the Advocate, the Holy Spirit, whom the Father will send in my name, will teach you all things and will remind you of everything I have said to you." (The *Merriam-Webster Dictionary* defines an advocate as a counselor or "one who pleads the cause of another."[11]) Notice the two words that Jesus used: all things. That means there is nothing too big or too small for

---

11 "Advocate Definition & Meaning," *Merriam-Webster*, https://www.merriam-webster.com/dictionary/advocate.

the Holy Spirit. He will teach you all things as He leads you into the peaceful, powerful, joy-filled life Jesus came to give you.

First John 2:27 (NLT) says it this way:

But you have received the Holy Spirit, and he lives within you, so you don't need anyone to teach you what is true. For the Spirit teaches you everything you need to know, and what he teaches is true—it is not a lie. So just as he has taught you, remain in fellowship with Christ.

The Holy Spirit is in you and will teach you everything you need to know. And what He teaches you is truth! Your spirit recognizes and knows truth. Your Bible is going to start coming alive because God's Spirit is your teacher.

The Holy Spirit is your guide, according to John 16:13 (NIV): "But when he, the spirit of truth, comes, he will guide you into all truth. He will not speak on his own: he will speak only what he hears, and he will tell you what is to come." Some of you are trying to figure out what you're supposed to do. That's one of the roles of the Holy Spirit—He wants to guide you, as can be seen in Isaiah 30:21 (NIV), "Whether you turn to the right or to the left, your ears will hear a voice behind you, saying, 'This is the way; walk in it.'"

If you want to experience a greater encounter with the Holy Spirit, you just need to ask Him. Say, "Holy Spirit, show me! Reveal Yourself to me!" I pray this every day. *Holy Spirit, show me. Give me wisdom. Show me what to do, and even show me where to go. Show me—me! Holy Spirit, show me!* In Ezekiel 36:26-27 (NIV), God says, "I will give you a new heart and put a new spirit in you: I will remove from you your heart of stone and give you a heart of flesh." [In other words, He's going to go from an external God to an internal God.] "And I will put my Spirit in you and move you to follow my decrees and be careful to keep my laws."

One of the most powerful things you can do to invite the Holy Spirit into your life is to pray scripture. The psalmist David said, "Search me, God, and know my heart; test me and know my anxious thoughts. See if there is any offensive way in me, and lead me in the way of everlasting" (Psalm 139:23-24, NIV). In other words, find something in me that offends You, and lead me in a way that will last. You don't need to go down the wrong path that will cause you to waste time and feel unnecessary pain—not when you have a Teacher and a Guide who's in you to lead you into an abundant life!

People spend years wondering and questioning if they are going in the right direction with their lives: *Did I pick the right career? Did I marry the right spouse? Where should I go to college? What church should I attend? I've waited so long to get married, and even though there are red flags, I'm going through with it, and God will change them.*

If you pray scripture, you won't need me or anybody else telling you what's right or wrong. You'll be making room for the Holy Spirit in your life. Let me say it this way. To every one of you who is tired of even trying to be a Christian . . . wouldn't it be better if when you tried to do it, there was something in you moving you to want to do it? That's what happens when you say, "Holy Spirit, show me . . . do the work inside of me." Then, after you ask the Holy Spirit to show you, ask Him to change you.

"Holy Spirit, change me."

Once you've asked the Holy Spirit to change your heart, it's incredibly important that you don't stay where you started. Take spiritual steps. You said, "I have decided to follow Jesus." You know what's going to happen every time you take steps? You're going to grow. You can say, "I'm not where I want to be, but I'm not where I used to be either." And, you'll grow! Second Corinthians 3:17-18 (NLT) says:

For the Lord is the Spirit, and wherever the Spirit of the Lord is, there is freedom. So all of us who have had that veil removed can see and reflect the glory of the Lord. And the Lord—who is the Spirit—makes us more and more like him as we are changed into his glorious image.

Wherever He is, there's a breath of fresh air, and wherever that breath of fresh air is—wherever you're allowing Him to work in your life—freedom happens! But you have to give Him permission. "Holy Spirit, show me." "Holy Spirit, change me." And the last thing you can say is "Holy Spirit, fill me. In other words, give me everything you have." Tell the Lord you want more. Tell Him, "I want more of your work in my life. Fill me."

The Bible says in Acts 13:52 (NASB, 1995) that the disciples were "continually filled with joy and with the Holy Spirit," and throughout the book of Acts, they get filled and refilled again and again. Why? Because God has more. Simply put, I want you—over these next few weeks—to pray, "Holy Spirit, show me ways I can grow. Show me things that are offending you. Holy Spirit, change me. I want to be more like you. Holy Spirit, fill me. I'm ready to go all in."

Scan to download the song from this chapter.

PRAYER

Holy Spirit, I invite You into my life. I pray You would abide in me and rest upon me as I go about my day. I want to be led by Your voice and empowered by Your strength. My greatest desire is to know You intimately as my teacher and friend. You are welcome in my heart, my home, and every aspect of my life. I need Your wisdom to guide and direct me in every decision I make. Holy Spirit, You have control of my life, and I will trust and obey Your voice. In Jesus's name. Amen.

TWENTY-THREE

DECLARATION SONG (DECLARE THE GOODNESS OF OUR GOD)

♪

Shout for victory
Sing for breakthrough
Dance for freedom

Declare the goodness of our God
Jesus is the answer
Declare the goodness of our God

MUSIC AND LYRICS BY MARTHA MUNIZZI & DAVID OUTING

According to the Merriam-Webster Dictionary, to declare means, "to state emphatically; to make known formally, officially, or explicitly."[12] It also means to state out loud a fact; to issue an authoritative command.

Did you know your mind listens to the words you use? Your mind does what it thinks you want it to do. Your mind's job is not to keep you happy but rather to keep you alive. Your mind has no choice but to listen to the words you tell it. Your mind is always switched on. It's always recording. It never pauses or goes into "sleep mode." When we feel frustrated and overwhelmed, sometimes we start saying things

---

12 Merriam-Webster.com Dictionary, s.v. "declare," https://www.merriam-webster.com/dictionary/declare.

like, "If I don't get that raise, I think I'll lose it!" or, "This commute to work will be the death of me," or, "I am dying under all this paperwork!" Your mind is actually listening to what you think is killing you. "If I get rejected again, I'll die!" "It'll kill me if I don't get that promotion!" "I won't be able to handle it if things don't change soon!" Your mind listens to what you tell it and starts to give you internal feedback based on those words. It has no choice but to listen to the words you use. Expert studies trace negativity to sicknesses like high blood pressure. So your job is to feed your mind better words, more positive thoughts—thoughts in line with God's Word. Changing your language can change your reality. It sounds simple, but the results are profound. Your situation can change as quickly as you change your language. God needs your language to change before your situation can change.

God's Word will have a powerful impact on you if you believe it, but releasing our faith isn't only about praying and believing. It also has a lot to do with our speaking. It has to do with the words we say every single day. When you read your Bible every day, it's strengthening you. It's healing you. It's making you new. But you need to declare God's promises over your life and get in agreement with what He has said about you in His word! Transformation happens when you get into agreement with the truth of God's Word. Prayer will bring you into agreement with what God said, but worship is agreement with who God is. He is Jehovah Rapha my healer; Jehovah Jireh my provider, Jehovah Shalom, my peace! Make sure there is more prayer and praise coming out of your mouth more often than negativity, and declare God's goodness in every situation!

When my mother recently recovered from a shoulder and hip injury, she went to the doctor for her post-surgery check-up after several months of healing. I went with her to hear the doctor's diagnosis of her progress. Mom had been favoring the broken areas for weeks. She knew her body was healing, but she still was being very careful with her right side to protect against further injury. Although she was no longer in pain, instead of walking normally, she would limp as well as lean on me for support. When we arrived at her doctor's appointment, I helped her out of her car and carefully helped her walk into the doctor's office. After her evaluation, the doctor told her the good news. "Faith, I noticed when you came into my office today you were babying the side of your body that was broken. You don't have to favor that side anymore because those bones have healed completely. Go ahead and start moving and walking normally because you are healed. You are stronger now in those areas than you were before your accident because there are steel rods inside your body where the injuries were. Right now, you are as healed as you're ever going to be." It was the news my mother was praying to hear! She got up and walked out of the doctor's office without leaning on me and walking straighter than she had in months. That's how powerful words are!

> *When you read your Bible every day, it's strengthening you. It's healing you. It's making you new.*

Every day, we are bombarded by the media with an onslaught of negativity, arguments, and divisive words. We hear words that trigger our emotions, stir up our fears, and cause us to think the situation we may be facing is hopeless. We need to use God's Word to cut through all the lies of the enemy! The truth we believe is not determined by what our culture has deemed true based on convenience. No! God's

Word is our foundation! It is our anchor, and it will stand the test of time! It doesn't matter what CNN says. It doesn't matter what Fox News thinks. It doesn't matter what MSNBC's opinion is. The only thing that matters is what God's Word says—and it is filled with so many good and precious promises. It is our unshakeable foundation. We can stand on it, and it will not fail! It will cut through lies, deception, offense, and feelings of unworthiness, and if you live by it, it will make you stronger! You've probably heard the statement, "The truth will set you free, but first it will make you miserable." Freedom can be painful. It's painful to let go of a relationship you realize is not God's best for you. It's painful to admit you were hurt by someone, and you've allowed offense to keep you from reconciling, losing years of relationship with that person. It hurts your flesh when you start tithing and giving, when you really need that money to pay bills, but you want to obey God and grow in your faith. But that pain is producing something greater in you! It's shaping you! Every time you choose to obey God's Word, it will begin to work effectually in you and transform your life!

RESTRICTIONS NOT LIMITATIONS

My son, Nathan, recently had his right wrist crushed in a terrible car accident. It was the hand of God that protected him from something that could have been so much worse. His arm was in a cast for several weeks and, when the day came to have his cast removed, it was painful for him. His arm was healed after being placed in a cast, but even though the bones and ligaments had healed, he still experienced pain. But the pain is the proof that freedom is close. The restriction of the brace is what kept his arm from further injury.

Every time you choose to obey God's Word, it will begin to work effectually in you and transform your life!

The Bible comes with restrictions but not limitations. You're not giving up anything by giving everything to Jesus. His Word is the only guide we'll ever need. It is life! It is freedom! It's protection! A life shaped by God's Word is a life that will stand strong through every trial!

GOD'S WORD IS A WEAPON

You and I are in a spiritual battle for our victory and we fight with weapons that are not of this world. We can use God's Word as a weapon to fight everything coming against us by speaking it every day. The Bible says in Ps 149:5-6 (NKJV), "Let the saints be joyful in glory; Let them sing aloud on their beds. Let the high praises of God be in their mouth, and a two-edged sword in their hand." And Hebrews 4:12 (NIV) tells us, "For the word of God is alive and active. Sharper than any double-edged sword, it penetrates even to dividing soul and spirit, joints and marrow: it judges the thoughts and attitudes of the heart."

What is the meaning of a two-edged sword? Have you ever prayed about a situation, and then suddenly a scripture comes to your mind? At that moment, you know instantly that God has given you a verse to stand on and to claim over your situation. What's happening is God has given you a "Rhema" word (which is how God talks to us personally one-on-one), and it's a word that is so sharp that when your spirit hears it, it cuts right through your questions, intellect, and natural logic.

The phrase "two-edged" is taken from the Greek word *distomos*. It's a compound of the word *di*, meaning two, and the word *stomos*, which is the Greek word for one's mouth. When these two words are compounded together (*distomos*), it means two-mouthed!

After you meditated on that *rhema*, or that quickened word from God, it suddenly begins to release its power inside of you. Soon you couldn't contain it any longer! Everything within you wanted to declare what God had said to you. When you spoke God's word out of your mouth, it went forth like a powerful blade to drive back the forces of hell that had been coming against you.

When you get a *rhema* word from God, you immediately know that you have to do more than just believe it, you have to declare it and release it out of your mouth! How does it become a two-edged sword? When the word initially came out of God's mouth it created one side of the sword. But when you come into agreement by declaring it out of your mouth, another blade is added to the sword and it becomes a "two-edged" or a "two-mouthed" sword! God's word is powerful when it's spoken!

If God speaks something it WILL come to pass. We have God's promise found in Luke 1:37 (AMP), "For with God nothing is ever impossible and no word from God shall be without power or impossible of fulfillment."

Whatever you need that you don't yet have, praise God for it now. Praising God binds our enemies and brings God's Word to pass. Praising God is the activator for the presence and power of God. Your praise always brings God onto the scene!

Psalm 68:1 (NIV) says, "May God arise, may his enemies be scattered", and Psalm 8:2 (NIV) says, "Through the praise of children and infants you have established a stronghold against your enemies, to silence the foe and the avenger." God has ordained your mouth for victory! God has ordained your mouth to stop His enemies.

And if that's not enough to encourage you to keep declaring the promises of God, the bible also says that God, Himself, stands over and watches over His own Word, making sure it is fulfilled. Jeremiah 1:12 (AMP) says, "Then said the Lord to me, You have seen well, for I am alert and active, watching over My word to perform it." The KJV says, "For I will hasten my word to perform it." The NKJV says, "For I am ready to perform My word." The NIV says, "For I am watching to see that my word is fulfilled" and the ERV says, "I am watching to make sure that my message to you comes true."

To all who are reading this today, meditate on these words found in Job 22:28 (NKJV), "You will also declare a thing, and it will be estab- *Scan to download the song from this chapter.* lished for you; So, light will shine on your ways." Declare a thing and it will be established! Every chance you get, declare how good your God is! When the enemy comes against you, shout unto God for your victory. When you need a miracle, sing for your breakthrough. In sickness and in health, declare the goodness of your God. With or without a job, shout His praises. Let everything that has breath praise the Lord! Declare the goodness of God every day and God will shine on your ways!

PRAYER

Lord Jesus, Your goodness knows no bounds. Your goodness is greater than anything I can imagine or explain. No matter how difficult my situation may be, I refuse to remain in a place of despair because I know all things are working out for my good! Today, I will use my voice to sing and shout how good, how powerful, and how mighty You are. I will declare favor and breakthrough in my life because Your promises are Yes and Amen! In Jesus' name. Amen!

TWENTY-FOUR

FIGHT FOR ME

♪

You fight for me
You fight for me
You turn praises to victory
You fight for me
You fight for me
Every battle you've won

I won't worry
I don't have to be afraid
You fight for me
I can walk in victory
I'm not leaning on my
own strength
I am holding onto your way
Walkin' in victory
I'm walkin' in victory

MUSIC AND LYRICS BY DANIELLE MUNIZZI & DAVID OUTING

After waiting almost ten years to release new music, I started to sense it was time to record a live album in 2020. The year 2020 was crazy for all of us, but I felt like God wanted me to start writing again. The songs started coming together quickly for this record, and from the time we started the writing process, it was less than thirty days before we'd recorded a brand new live album, *Best Days*, at our home church in Orlando, EpicLife.

"Fight For Me" is one of my favorite songs on the Best Days album and was written by my oldest daughter, Danielle Munizzi and our producer David Outing. The song was originally written as a ballad, but when Danielle sang it for our producer, he heard something different. He completely changed the feel of the song from a slow one to a fast one—and we loved it! "Fight for Me" went on to become our first radio single in 2021 that ended up on the Top 30 charts on gospel radio. And because of this song, I won Traditional Female Artist of the Year at the 2022 Stellar Awards.

One day, during a radio interview, a man named Joe called in to share his testimony of how God used "Fight For Me" to encourage him through a difficult struggle he had just experienced. He said the song impacted him so much and reminded him of how God covers us and fights for us when the enemy attacks our lives. He shared that, when he was a little boy, he would get bullied on the playground at school. Every day, a bully would push him around and try to beat him up. Joe would tell the mean kid every day, "If you don't stop bullying me, I'll tell my older brother, and you do not want him to show up here. He's crazy! There's no telling what he'll do to you!" Joe's big brother, who had been in trouble a lot in his life, was a little crazy. This went on for a few days until Joe had had enough. One day, when the bad kid showed up, Joe's crazy older brother came to defend his little brother. The bully was no match for his bigger, badder, crazier older brother, and he never bothered him again after that!

Did you know the Bible calls Jesus our older brother? When the enemy attacks you, your older brother, Jesus, has got your back! He is fighting for you and defeating the bullies in your life that try to harass and intimidate you. This is a truth that will set you free from worry, fear, and anxiety if you believe it.

Exodus 14:14 (NIV) says, "The Lord will fight for you; you need only to be still." God will always do His part to keep His promises to you, when we do our part by using the weapons of worship and praise to defeat the enemy. The Bible tells us God's power is released when we worship, and He will use that power against our enemies to defeat them!

> *Did you know the Bible calls Jesus our older brother? When the enemy attacks you, your older brother has got your back! He is fighting for you and defeating the bullies in your life that try to harass and intimidate you. This is a truth that will set you free from worry, fear, and anxiety if you believe it.*

Our weapons are not physical.

We have weapons that work to pull back the curtain of the enemy's lies, not just to fight the symptoms of those lies. We have been handed God's armor.

We don't use natural weapons to fight.

2 Corinthians 10:3-4 (NIV) says, "For though we live in the world, we do not wage war as the world does. The weapons we fight with are not the weapons of the world. On the contrary, they have divine power to demolish strongholds."

We have all the weapons we need to win! As believers, we are equipped with the most sophisticated spiritual tactical gear in the world. In the hands of operators that know how to use their weapons, this advantage over the enemy is huge!

Ephesians 6:10-18 (NIV) says:

Finally, be strong in the Lord and in his mighty power. Put on the full armor of God, so that you can take your stand against the devil's schemes. For our struggle is not against flesh and blood, but against the rulers, against the authorities, against the powers of this dark world and against the spiritual forces of evil in the heavenly realms. Therefore put on the full armor of God, so that when the day of evil comes, you may be able to stand your ground, and after you have done everything, to stand. Stand firm then, with the belt of truth buckled around your waist, with the breastplate of righteousness in place, and with your feet fitted with the readiness that comes from the gospel of peace. In addition to all this, take up the shield of faith, with which you can extinguish all the flaming arrows of the evil one. Take the helmet of salvation and the sword of the Spirit, which is the word of God. And pray in the Spirit on all occasions with all kinds of prayers and requests.

This is how faith that drives out fear is developed. The Word of God is the sword of the Spirit. Speak the Word of God. Use it to fight Satan every time he comes against you. Hold up your shield of faith and quench all his fiery darts. Speak words of faith, and fear will depart.

Rebuke fear. Whenever you feel fear trying to come upon you, don't stand it for a moment. Say, "Fear, I rebuke you in Jesus's name. Now go!"

Whenever you're tempted to be in fear, anxiety or worry, immediately begin to pray in the Spirit. It will edify your inner man and bring supernatural peace.

Deuteronomy 20:4 (ERV) says, "The Lord your God is going with you to help you fight against your enemies. He will help you win!"

When you see the enemy coming against you, don't waver in unbelief. Don't fear. Don't hesitate. Don't panic. God—your God—is right there with you, fighting against your enemies—fighting to win.

This is our victory!

Here's the truth: the victory is irrevocable.

The victory has already been given—we win!

Scan to download the song from this chapter.

PRAYER

Lord Jesus, I will not be afraid of any giant I might face today. Your Word says that You go before me, and You fight for me, so I will not worry or fear. Thank You for giving me the strength to overcome all my enemies today. I rebuke all anxiety, depression, and fear that may try to overtake me. I know the battle belongs to You, and because of You, I have the victory! Thank You, Jesus! Amen.

TWENTY-FIVE

LIFT HIM UP

♪

Give Him the highest praise
For He is worthy to be lifted up
Give Him the highest praise
For He is worthy to be lifted up

Worthy, worthy, worthy
He is worthy to be lifted up

Worthy, worthy, worthy
He is worthy to be lifted up

Lift Him up!
Lift Him up!
Lift Him up!

MUSIC AND LYRICS BY MARTHA MUNIZZI

Several years ago, a very close friend of mine experienced the devastating loss of her fourteen-year-old son in a horrific car accident. I got the phone call that he had been in an accident and that it was serious, but I wasn't sure of his condition until I got to the hospital.

When I walked into the emergency room, the nurse brought me to the room where my friend had just received the fateful news. She had her back to the door, so she didn't see me come in. I knew by her posture and her deep cries of grief that he had passed away. I wrapped my arms around her and sat with her, and we cried together. She couldn't see me through her massive tears, but she leaned into my embrace.

A few moments later, a nurse came in and asked us to move out into the lobby, so they could move his body from the emergency room. My friend and I—and several other friends and family members—walked into the lobby to avoid seeing what would have been too devastating for any of us to handle.

As we walked into the lobby, my friend broke away from my arms and ran outside into the parking lot. We all ran out after her to make sure she wasn't running into oncoming traffic in her gut-wrenching grief. We watched in amazement as she ran through the parking lot, shouting as loud as she could, "God, I love You! I will never stop praising You! You can take everything on this earth away from me, and I will never stop thanking You for all You have done for me. I love You, Jesus! I praise You, Jesus! I trust You with my life!"

I remember being stunned and thinking, *How can she praise God with such complete abandon, with no concern over who is watching her, in one of the darkest moments of her entire life? How is she running and jumping and thanking God when she just lost her son?* Where did she find the strength? As I watched her, I started to ask myself if I could have done that. If I'm being honest, I don't know if I could praise God like she did after experiencing that kind of devastating loss.

That moment was a turning point for me. If I was going to lead others in worship, I had to go deeper in my own worship. Worshiping God during the darkest moments of our lives is true worship!

The question is a tough one, but for you and me to grow in our worship, it needs to be asked: Can you praise God in your night season? We may never experience the excruciating loss of a child or a loved one, but we will have night seasons.

When you sing a song of faith in your night season, it shows that you believe God's Word to you to be true, and you trust Him to fulfill it. A song of faith in the night is the highest form of praise. You attract Him through praise because your praise shows that you have faith.

Hebrews 11:6 (NIV) says, "And without faith it is impossible to please God because anyone who comes to Him must believe that He exists and that He rewards those who earnestly seek Him."

> *When you sing a song of faith in your night season, it shows you believe God's Word to you to be true, and you trust Him to fulfill it. A song of faith in the night is the highest form of praise. You attract Him through praise because your praise shows that you have faith.*

God is worthy of our worship in the darkest moments of our life.

Psalm 16:7 (NKJV) says, "I will bless the Lord who has given me counsel; my heart also instructs me in the night seasons." God is speaking during your night season! That's why worship is so critical to getting through your pain.

He is worthy to be praised no matter what we're going through. Our circumstances should never dictate our worship. No matter how bad the season might be that we are in, God is—and will always be— worthy of our highest and best praise.

When you get a revelation that God deserves praise no matter your circumstances, it changes your pattern of thinking which will change your pattern of behavior.

That's when you will stop being moved by what you see. Worship will become a natural part of your life—and, ultimately, who you are.

It's easy to praise God when things are going your way. Learn to go beyond that. Learn to give God praise even when all hell is breaking loose around you. Learn to give God praise when your heart is broken. Give God your worship when you can't pay your bills or when you face betrayal from someone you love. Give God praise when life disappoints you, and things don't go the way you thought they would. Sing a song in the night when you're discouraged and depleted of strength, and the enemy is whispering to you to give up and telling you no one cares about you. That's when you give God a higher praise! A greater praise! A praise of which He is worthy!

Thanksgiving and praise are power twins. Thanksgiving releases joy, and praise releases God's power. When you can praise and thank God when everyone around you thinks you should give up, that's when you begin to experience the presence of God, the power of God, the love of God and the mercy of God on a level you've never experienced before. Praise will unlock a greater revelation of who God is and reveal more of His character.

My friend suffered the worst loss imaginable, but that wasn't the end of the story. She told me a few years later that her relationship with God was so much deeper and more intimate because of what she had gone through. She began to minister to people who had gone through similar tragedies, and her experience became a tool God used to bring hope and healing to others. Her pain became her passion. Her misery became her message.

Lift Him up over your pain, your disappointments, your mistakes, and your past. In other words, put your focus

Scan to download the song from this chapter.

on Jesus and not on yourself. He is worthy to be praised in every circumstance; so, in your lowest moments, learn to give God your highest praise!

PRAYER

Father, with everything in me, I will praise You. I am filled with gratitude for the great things You have done for me. Today, I will give You my highest and best praise—not just with my words but with my actions. Thank You for the greater revelation unlocked in Your presence. I am overwhelmed by Your presence that comes when I worship. Today, I need Your love and mercy more than ever before, so I will give You my highest praise. In Jesus's name. Amen!

TWENTY-SIX

YOUR LATTER WILL BE GREATER

♪

*Your latter will be greater
than your past
You will be blessed—more
than you could ask
Despite all that has been done,
the best is yet to come
And your latter will be greater
Your latter will be greater
Your latter will be greater
than your past*

*All things are possible
Possible, possible, possible
All things are possible*

*Possible, possible, possible
And your latter will be greater,
Your latter will be greater,
your latter will be greater
than your past*

*The best is yet to come
The best is yet to come
Oh, the best is yet to come*

*The King is soon to come
The King is soon to come
Oh, the King is soon to come*

MUSIC AND LYRICS BY DERIK THOMAS & ISRAEL HOUGHTON

I didn't write this song, but from the first time I heard it, I knew it would be my anthem. It was the song that pulled me through difficult moments of intense doubt and uncertainty. After almost a decade of serving in our local church, God was changing our assignment—one that we loved—and requiring us to move way out of our comfort zone into a place of blind faith.

"Your latter will be greater!" I declared as I sobbed, worried that what was ahead for us wasn't greater than what we were leaving behind. I had big dreams but almost no resources. I was praying for greater opportunities but looking at a lot of closed doors. I was worried about the future because all I could see was the present! If you had seen my situation then, you would have been worried for me too! Accomplishing any of my dreams was a long shot and actually seemed more like a fantasy than real life.

I was willing to let go of what I wanted to hold onto. I was willing to trust God, but I needed to know He was going to give me back more than I was giving up!

The book of Job tells the story of a man of great wealth living in the land of Uz with his large family and many livestock. The Bible says Job was "blameless" and "upright," always careful to avoid doing evil (1:1). One day, Satan ("the adversary") appeared before God in heaven. God boasted to Satan about Job's goodness, but Satan argued Job was only good because God had blessed him abundantly. Satan challenged God and claimed that if he were given permission to punish the man, Job would turn and curse God.

God allowed Satan to torment Job to test this bold claim, but He forbade Satan to take Job's life in the process. Job lost everything: his children, his land, and his livestock. As if that weren't bad enough, Job became covered in sores as part of Satan's test. Job had a lot of negative friends who encouraged him to curse God, so he could die in peace. His friends gave him terrible spiritual advice, his wife told him to curse God and die, but Job refused to blame God.

A lot happens in 42 chapters, and it's definitely worth reading the entire story.

The test started when Job, at seventy years old, lost everything. He lived another 120 years, which means he was 210 years old when he died. Before he died, his children were restored: God gave him seven more sons and three more daughters. He lived to see the fourth generation of his family. His latter was so much greater than his past! His final years were so much better than his beginning! God restored everything Job had lost with even more than he'd had before! That's the nature of God! He will restore everything the enemy has stolen out of your life.

Take a look at Job 8:7 in multiple translations:

1) "Though your beginning was small, your end will increase greatly." (MEV)

2) "Then what you had in the past will seem small compared with the great prosperity you'll have in the future." (GW)

3) "And though you started with little, you will end with much." (NLT)

4) "Your future will be brighter by far than your past." (CEV)

5) "Your former state will seem inconsequential in the light of your future prosperity." (NCB)

6) "Where you began will seem unimportant because your future will be so successful." (NCV)

7) "In the past, things went well with you. But in days to come, things will get even better." (NIrV)

Every translation is so empowering and encouraging. Don't look at where you are or what you're going through. Trust that God knows what you're going through, and He will cause you to be successful. Your future is going to be so much better than your past! Don't be discouraged, and don't give up! Get your hopes up because what's coming is greater!

> *Don't look at where you are or what you're going through. Trust that God knows what you're going through, and He will cause you to be successful. Your future is going to be so much better than your past!*

Your latter will be greater than your past. You will be blessed more than you could ask. Despite all that has been done, the best is yet to come! And your latter will be greater than the rest!

All things are possible! What's ahead of you is so much better than what's behind you! Stop looking back, and start believing that better things are ahead for you! No matter what you've gone through, don't let the past stop you from moving into your future. Greater blessings are coming. Better days are ahead! Start speaking it! Get your hopes up! Expect more— more miracles, more healings, and greater breakthroughs!

Scan to download the song from this chapter.

PRAYER

Jesus, I thank You that my best days are ahead of me. I cut ties with whatever is behind me, and I reach forward to the prize set before me, and I believe and declare that the best is yet to come! In Jesus' name, Amen!

TWENTY-SEVEN

JESUS IS THE BEST THING (THAT EVER HAPPENED TO ME)

♪

Jesus is the best thing that
ever happened to me
Jesus is the best thing that
ever happened to me

Oh, He took my old life
and gave me new life
All that I'd done wrong,
He made it so right
Took me from darkness
into the sunlight
When I was nothing, He
turned me into something

Jesus is the best thing that
ever happened to me
Jesus is the best thing that
ever happened to me

With only one touch, He
gave me so much
I don't deserve it—He
said I was worth it
He gives me joy and He
makes me happy
He showed me a better way,
and now I've got to say

MUSIC AND LYRICS BY MARTHA MUNIZZI

A fter twenty-five years of marriage, my parents divorced. My mother wouldn't sign the divorce papers for almost a year. My sisters and I had to give her an ultimatum because unfortunately we knew my Dad was never going to change his heart. We told her she had to sign the papers, move on, and put my father and her broken marriage into God's hands. We told her if she couldn't move on, then it was going to affect her relationships with her daughters. We knew God had a better plan for her, and He wanted to reveal it to her, but she had to let go. She sobbed at the thought of divorce because she felt like a failure. Finally, she agreed to sign the papers and be officially divorced.

Six days after she signed the papers, our cousin called one of my sisters with some shocking news. My cousin said, "Well, I guess congratulations are in order." My sister had no idea what she meant and asked her to explain. "Your Dad just got married!" Needless to say, we were shocked that so quickly after the divorce had been made official, my father had already remarried. Now we understood why my Dad hadn't even discussed reconciliation with my mother. He had already moved on with someone else. It was heartbreaking for my mother, but she had decided to put her heartbreak into God's hands and trust Him with her future.

The grief of a divorce is unlike any other pain because it feels like a death. It actually is a type of death: the death of a family unit—the death of dreams still to come. It's very difficult to overcome a broken marriage because a part of you is gone. It was difficult for my sisters and me, as well, because we had to get used to the reality that my parents weren't going to grow old together. My father had found someone else with whom to live out his older years, but our concern was for our mother. What was her future going to look like? She was hurting and angry, but she was never angry at God.

She knew God hadn't failed her—my father had. God didn't leave her—my father did. She cried herself to sleep at night, but she knew in her heart that God was going to restore her broken heart.

My mother stayed faithful to God and faithful to her local church. She is a phenomenally gifted piano and organ player, and she never stopped leading worship, even though she was hurting. One day, a man in the audience saw my Mom onstage at her church playing the piano. He hadn't really noticed her before, but on this day, he did. His wife had recently passed away, and he thought he would never remarry. He prayed a prayer and said to God, "If by some chance I ever get married again, I would love to marry someone like that woman on the piano."

He said God spoke and whispered in his ear, "Why not her?" A few days later, he talked to her pastor and asked if he could invite her to coffee. My mother's pastor and a few of the women of the church were very protective of her and hadn't let anyone close to her up to that point. The man asked her pastor for his permission, took her to coffee, and the rest is history. They fell in love and were married for twenty-five years until he went home to be with the Lord. Not only was he the love of her life—he also became an amazing father to us and a grandfather to our children. God is a restorer!

Looking back on that time in our lives and other tragic moments that shook our family to its core, I can say that Jesus is the best thing that has ever happened to me!

God kept us and provided for us way beyond what we could have imagined. He kept us through divorce, sexual abuse, brokenness, lack, sickness, cancer, and more. My family never would have made it through the storms we faced without Jesus. Through struggles and heartbreak, we learned that Jesus will recover everything that was stolen and bless us one thousand times more! Yes, there have been times we've had to deal with confusion, loss, and pain, but there have also been so many seasons of incredible opportunities, blessings, and open doors. I've had the chance to meet a lot of incredibly talented and gifted people in my life, but I can unequivocally say knowing Jesus is better!

I couldn't make it through life without Jesus.

1 John 4:10 (TPT) says, "This is love: He loved us long before we loved him. It was his love, not ours. He proved it by sending his Son to be the pleasing sacrificial offering to take away our sins."

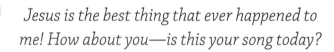

Jesus is the best thing that ever happened to me! How about you—is this your song today?

Jesus is the best thing that ever happened to me! How about you— is this your song today? Can you sing that He is the best thing even during the storms and in spite of what is happening around you? What about when fear invades your mind, storms beat you up, and rains beat you down? Believe me, I understand that this life can be brutal, but despite all these storms, we are more than conquerors, overcomers, and victorious warriors through Christ who loves us. Jesus is the Lord of the storm. Even the winds and waves obey Him. Jesus is our shelter from the wind and our refuge from the storm!

Thank you, Jesus! You are the best thing that ever happened to me! Choose to place your faith, future, family, finances, fears, failures, and frustrations in our Father's hands. He is our All-Sovereign, All-Powerful, All-Loving, All-Knowing, Almighty, Faithful, Forgiving, Unfailing, Unchangeable, Immovable, Unshakable God! Today, I pray we will choose to believe Him and receive His love, His goodness, and His comfort. He will save, sustain, deliver,

Scan to download the song from this chapter.

restore, heal, and help. He will provide, transform, and use us, and everything we go through will bring Him glory.

Scripture contains more than a dozen "better than" statements. What's better than fame? Wealth? Even life itself? The answer is Jesus! The best thing I did was put my faith in God and trust Him with my life. I wouldn't be who I am today had I not made the choice to completely rely on Him no matter how hard my situation was.

No matter what, I am committed to my testimony: "Jesus is the best thing that ever happened to me!"

PRAYER

Jesus, following You was the best decision of my life. I am so grateful for the blessings You have bestowed on my life. You have provided me with more than I ever could have imagined. Thank You for Your unconditional love and for showing me just how great that love is by sending Christ to die for me. Thank You for all You've done, all You're doing, and all You're going to do! In Jesus's name. Amen.

TWENTY-EIGHT

BEST DAYS

♪

These are the best days
He's doing a new thing
You bring rivers to the dry land
And water to the wasteland

These are the best days
He's doing his best work
Do you know it?
Do you see it?
Just trust Him and believe it

I'm changing my perspective
I'll keep my eyes on Jesus
I'm standing on Your promise
I'll keep my eyes on Jesus

Oh, I'm standing on promises
You don't let down
No, you don't forget
Though I'm waiting
I know what you said
These are the best days

You're doing a new thing

I'll keep my eyes on Jesus
It's breaking out before me
I'll keep my eyes on Jesus

You don't let down
No, you don't forget
Though I'm waiting
I know what you said
These are the best days
You're doing a new thing

I'm changing my perspective
I'll keep my eyes on Jesus
I'm standing on Your promise
I'll keep my eyes on Jesus

I see the cross before me
I'll keep my eyes on You
I'll leave the world behind me
I'll keep my eyes on You

MUSIC AND LYRICS BY MARTHA MUNIZZI, DANIELLE MUNIZZI, NICOLE MUNIZZI, DAVID OUTING

I saiah 43:19 (MSG) says, "Be alert, be present. I'm about to do something brand-new. It's bursting out! Don't you see it? There it is! I'm making a road through the desert, rivers in the badlands."

This is not the story of a people who were living the high life. On the contrary, they had been wandering for forty years when they were actually only eleven days' walking distance from their promised land. What happened? Why did it take them so long? The Bible says they murmured and complained. Their griping kept them in unbelief, which kept them wondering and wandering. That can so easily happen to us if we're not intentional about where we put our focus. There's an old saying: "The devil doesn't care what ditch you fall into as long as you get off the road."

Another way to apply this verse is to say, "God is doing a new thing, and it's springing forth now." When is now? Now is whenever you decide to get into agreement and alignment with God and His Word and start cooperating with Him—that's when *now* starts! The definition of the word now is "at the present time or moment."[13] It also means, "the time immediately to follow." I even looked up the synonyms for the word now, and they really make the point. Thesaurus.com says now can be replaced with the following: at this moment, straightaway, at-once, instantly, at this time, right now, and right away.[14] Faith is action, and it starts now!

Stop worrying now! Stop complaining and murmuring now! Start seeing your future through God's perspective now! You don't have to wait—you can do all of these things right now!

Hebrews 11:1 (NKJV) tells us, "Now faith is the substance of things hoped for, the evidence of things not seen." You're not always going

---

13 "Now Definition & Meaning," *Merriam-Webster*, https://www.merriam-webster.com/dictionary/now.
14 "Synonyms of Now," www.thesaurus.com, https://www.thesaurus.com/browse/now.

to like what you see in the natural. You're going to have to see with eyes of faith if you want to see what God is doing.

The culture we live in is full of confusion, hurting people, and brokenness. We live in a world where people are experiencing so much emptiness and despair because of sin. So much of people's pain is self-inflicted, and if we see the world through the lens of its problems, it will only create frustration and strife towards those causing the pain, suffering, and division.

The political climate, racial unrest, gender confusion, divorce, Christians deconstructing their faith—it's all part of the spiritual battle we engage in daily. It's obvious we are under attack from the enemy. The natural response to attack would be to attack back and make people our enemy instead of seeing sin as the true enemy.

> *Your coworker is not your enemy. Your spouse is not your enemy. We only have one enemy, and he is already defeated. The world is bound by deception, and the enemy has lied to them. It's not our job to do anything but love them.*

If you see the world through the lens of the broken state it's in right now and buy into the vitriol that we hear every day in the media, it will only lead you to anger and frustration. Eventually, you will start to see people as your enemy instead of the real enemy, sin. Your coworker is not your enemy. Your spouse is not your enemy. We only have one enemy, and he is already defeated. The world is bound by deception, and the enemy has lied to them. It's not our job to do anything but love them.

Today is the best day to believe your son or daughter who might be far from God will experience a radical God

Scan to download the song from this chapter.

encounter. Don't let the enemy discourage you by what you see. Call out the God-given purpose in the person you love who is not living for God. Call out their destiny when you pray for them. Don't be angry at them—pray for them and love them. Use your authority to speak the truth over their lives! The love of Jesus is the only hope for the world, and if we will pray and seek the face of God, he will heal our land. God is going to heal your child. That's His promise to us. You may be going through some bad days, but I challenge you to look at it through a different lens.

Over the years, whenever I was having a bad day, my mother would say to me, "Martha, you're just going to have to learn how to turn your bad days into good days." She was right! I have spent years trying to master this principle, and it all starts with perspective. I can choose to see problems, or I can choose to see possibilities.

This is the day the Lord has made, and we will rejoice and be glad in it! Not tomorrow, not yesterday—today is the day to rejoice. Why? Because if you wait for a better day, you might miss the power of the moment. Right now, this moment, this day is your best day, and God is doing something new. Align your faith and believe that it's springing forth and bursting forth right now in your favor!

PRAYER

Jesus, forgive me for seeing my world through the lens of what's wrong more often than through the lens of what's right. Today, I stand on Isaiah 43, and I declare and believe that You are doing a new thing—it's bursting forth now! I believe You are doing a new thing in me, my family, and my future. These days are the best days! In Jesus's name. Amen.

TWENTY-NINE

EVERYTHING YOU DO IS A BLESSING

♪

I know You're in control of it all
My plans, my future, my call
You want good things for me
Things I can't see
You know the answer's
   on the way
The sun will shine again
You're working all things
   for my good
And for Your glory

Everything You do is a blessing
When You give or take away
The righteous are
   never forsaken

You are good in all Your ways

I know You're giving
   me the strength
To see another day
You're working all things
   for my good
And for Your glory, Your glory

My joy is a blessing
My test is a blessing
My pain is a blessing
You use it all to bless me

MUSIC AND LYRICS BY NICOLE MUNIZZI, MARTHA MUNIZZI, DANIELLE MUNIZZI, DAVID OUTING

"**M**om! I think I have a great idea for a song!"

One day, I was downstairs in my kitchen, and I could hear my daughter Nicole singing upstairs in her room. She, like so many others, experienced a season of grief and loss which she had struggled to overcome. For months, she had been working through her pain—so hearing her sing again really made me happy. She came running downstairs, out of breath, and began to sing the song she had just written. As she sang the words, I knew it was a song that I would record on my next album.

Everything You do is a blessing
When You give and take away
The righteous are never forsaken
You are good in all Your ways

I love the message of this song. It describes to us just how much we can rely on God and trust His ways. God never fails! He is always good! Psalm 145:17-19 Easy-to-Read Version says, "Everything the Lord does is good. Everything he does shows how loyal he is."

When I was in my twenties, I worked at Disney's Hollywood Studios in Orlando. I was a member of a four-part girls' singing group that sang 40s and 50s music as part of the "Streetmosphere" character improvisational cast. We worked through the Thanksgiving and Christmas holidays, spending the days walking through the park, singing songs and performing improvisational skits to entertain the guests. We learned a lot of acting tips from the other cast members. One of the most important tips we learned was the "Yes and, rule."

We were told that, if we were going to be any good at improve, we had to follow the "Yes and, rule." The Yes and, rule is one of the basic tenets of improv comedy, and it's a protocol that allows for anything to happen. Whatever your fellow actors present to you, your response must always be yes. No matter what it is, you are required to agree and say yes. Instead of negating it, belittling it, or disagreeing with it, your job is to say, "Yes, and. . . ." Accept the scenario as it's presented to you (regardless of where you wanted it to go), and then add to it.

Let's say one improviser walks on stage and says their hair is on fire. Their teammate would then join them onstage and agree with that reality—that the first improviser's hair is indeed on fire. The first rule of improvisation is agree. Always agree and say yes. Let's say you and your acting partner are improvising and they say, "Freeze, I have a gun," and you say, "That's not a gun. It's your finger. You're pointing your finger at me." Our improvised scene has now ground to a halt. But if I say, "Freeze, I have a gun!" and you say, "The gun I gave you for Christmas?" Then we have started a scene because we have agreed that my finger is, in fact, a gun.

This may be a silly acting rule, but it's a very important spiritual principle for us to follow, as well. There are times when unexpected situations are thrown at you. Instead of complaining, just accept the scenario, no matter how challenging, and say yes! Sometimes, the biggest blessings come after the hardest tests. When God wants to bless you, He will take you through a testing season first. You can refuse and rebel if you want to, but I promise you, the test will come around again.

> *I don't always like the way God chooses to write my story, if I'm being honest, but I've learned that, instead of negating it, belittling it, disagreeing with it, or negotiating my way out of it, I need to say, "Yes, and. . . ."*

I don't always like the way God chooses to write my story, if I'm being honest, but I've learned that, instead of

Scan to download the song from this chapter.

negating it, belittling it, disagreeing with it, or negotiating my way out of it, I need to say, "Yes, and. . . ." My job is to accept the scenario as God presents it to me (regardless of how I wanted it to go) and then to add to it. Saying no will only shut down the story God is telling through your life. Your yes opens you up to more miracles. Your no will only shut down God's moment to shine in every test and trial you go through.

In improv, saying yes keeps the story alive and allows the other actors to add their parts to make the story more interesting. Your yes of obedience will allow God to continue writing your story. It's not always easy to say *yes* because we may not know what *yes* will require. Yes may look like letting go of something or someone we don't want to lose. Yes may look like you're going backward instead of forward. Yes may be saying no to what *you* want, so you can have what *God* wants. No matter what the situation may be, God will use every loss, every disappointment, every failure, and every mistake to bless you. He works all things together for the good of those who love Him and are called according to His purpose, according to Romans 8:28.

Don't miss the part about being called according to His purpose. His purpose is the only part of your story that matters. His purpose is the best part of your story, and it's the part people will read about and be impacted by.

Your story will have chapters of pain, hurt, disappointment, loss, and mistakes, but God promises He will use all of it to bless you. God has an incredible story He wants to write for your life. Quit trying to steal the pen! If you allow God to write your story, you will never be disappointed.

PRAYER

Jesus, I let go of everything I've been holding onto that has hindered Your blessings from coming into my life. Today, I give You the pen. I give You permission to write my story. I will say Yes to whatever You want me to do. I trust You with the parts of my story I don't understand, and I know You will use every part of it for my good. I want You to write the story and get the glory out of my life! Amen!

THIRTY

GOD IS HERE

♪

There is a sweet anointing
   in this sanctuary
There is a stillness in
   the atmosphere;
Come and lay down the
   burdens you have carried
For in the sanctuary,
   God is here

He is here
He is here to break the yoke

And lift the heavy burden
He is here
He is here to heal the
   hopeless heart
And bless the broken

Come and lay down the
   burdens you have carried
For in the sanctuary,
   God is here

MUSIC AND LYRICS BY MARTHA MUNIZZI, ISRAEL HOUGHTON, MELEASA HOUGHTON

D uring the writing process for my album, "The Best is Yet To Come" I had an idea to write a song called, "God is Here." I wanted to write a song about the Holy Spirit that described the presence of God in the room and what happens when He comes. I had one more writing session with my producer, and I knew that together we would work on the concept and finish writing the song collectively.

I flew to Nashville, Tennessee and my husband Dan and I met with my producer, Israel Houghton for our writing session, and the three of us gathered around a piano to pray and share ideas for new songs. As most songwriting sessions go, I started singing a melody with a few lines to a verse and a few other fragmented lyrics for "God is Here." Israel sat at the piano and began to play. He followed the notes that I was singing, searching for chords that would support (or go with) the melody. It wasn't long before more lyrics were crafted, and the song was beginning to take shape.

As we were brainstorming lyrics and chord structures and singing the few lines that we had written so far, we suddenly felt God's presence enter the room. The Holy Spirit was so strong that all three of us knew something powerful was happening. As Israel played the piano, I was so overwhelmed by what I was experiencing, I couldn't sing. All I wanted to do was fall on my knees and worship the Lord.

I don't know how long I stayed on my knees worshiping or how long that moment lasted, but none of us wanted it to end. We felt the tangible presence of the Holy Spirit fill the room before we even finished writing the song.

We finished writing the first two sections of "God is Here" that day but we weren't sure what we wanted to do for a bridge. Writing a bridge is very challenging because it has to "bridge" the other parts of the song together, but not take away from the main theme of the song. A bridge can add life to a song and if written well, can become the part everyone will remember the most. I know of a few songs where the bridge is my favorite part to sing!

We knew the verse and the chorus were special, so we proceeded carefully when considering adding the bridge. Since nothing was coming naturally, we agreed to give ourselves time and leave room for God to help us write something supernaturally.

During our final rehearsal, while we were rehearsing "God Is Here," we began to talk about what happens when the spirit of God invades our worship. The anointing of God breaks the yoke and lifts the burden. The words and melody to the bridge began to flow naturally and effortlessly and the song "God Is Here" was complete!

Over the years, I've had the awesome privilege of witnessing the impact this song has had in worship services all over the world. People have shared their incredible testimonies of how God came into the room while they were listening to this song and were healed of cancer, delivered from addictions, and experienced a supernatural encounter with the Lord.

> *Worship is the weapon that will release us from the bondage of the enemy and transforms us from being resistant 'to' worship, to using our worship as an act 'of' resistance. Worship is refusing to let whatever has upset us, confused us, or caused us fear, claim power over us.*

Leading people into the presence of God is one of my greatest passions. I love to see people experience the breakthrough God has for them through worship, and to discover a deeper connection with the Holy Spirit. Leading worship can be an amazing experience, but it can often be a challenge. When everyone is engaged and participating in the worship service, there's freedom, and you can feel the joy of the Lord in the room. I live for these moments!

But there are times when people come into a worship environment completely disinterested, staring at the worship team, distracted and unresponsive, and there's so much resistance it can feel like we're hitting a brick wall. There's no expression of freedom in worship because people are in bondage and burdened down by so many problems–physically, emotionally, and spiritually. Their present circumstances that bring fear, doubt, and anxiety have become a yoke around their neck and they can't break through those bondages to experience the freedom God's presence brings.

Worship is the weapon that will release us from the bondage of the enemy and transforms us from being resistant 'to' worship, to using our worship as an act 'of' resistance. Worship is refusing to let whatever has upset us, confused us, or caused us fear, claim power over us.

When the anointing is in the room, the presence of the Holy Spirit is present, and so is His power. In other words, when God shows up, everything He IS shows up with Him. Joy, peace, strength, freedom, healing, deliverance, salvation, and grace are all available when God's power is released in our worship. The job of the anointing is to break the yoke and lift the burden off of our life.

Isaiah 10:27 (KJV) says, "And it shall come to pass in that day, that his burden shall be taken away from off thy shoulder, and his yoke from off thy neck, and the yoke shall be destroyed because of the anointing."

In the book of Isaiah, the King of Assyria, an enemy of God's people, had set his sights on Judah. He captured her cities, demanded they pay taxes, and made a mockery of God. Hezekiah, the king of Judah, was desperate for help and went to the Temple to seek the Lord. The Lord sent the prophet Isaiah with a message to Hezekiah that God would lift the burden and destroy the yoke that had controlled and crushed them. God sent the prophet Isaiah with a message that He would set them free, and God did it because of the anointing!

Now, your enemy the devil has his sights set on you. What 'yoke' has the devil tried to place on you to hold you captive? Whether it be jealousy, fear, bitterness, hurt, pride, envy, or unforgiveness that weighs you down, you need the presence of God and His anointing to break the yoke, lift the burden, and set you free!

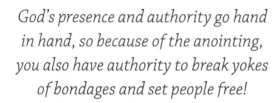

God's presence and authority go hand in hand, so because of the anointing, you also have authority to break yokes of bondages and set people free!

Your burden will be removed, and your yoke will be destroyed because of the anointing—not only the anointing of God's presence which is in the room, but the anointing that's on your life.

As you grow in your relationship with God, and begin to recognize His presence, the anointing will begin to rest on you more. And as a result, the anointing is now 'on' you to break yokes!

Luke 4:18-19 (NKJV) says, "The Spirit of the Lord is upon me, Because He has anointed Me to preach the gospel to the poor; He has sent Me to heal the brokenhearted, to proclaim freedom to the captives and recovery of sight to the blind, to set at liberty those who are oppressed; To proclaim the acceptable year of the Lord."

In these two verses, six things are mentioned as the result of the anointing of Christ. Three of them have to do with breaking bondages.

1) Heal the brokenhearted
2) Proclaim freedom to the captives
3) Bring liberty to those who are oppressed.

You and I have been given the anointing of the Holy Spirit and now we are "agents" of God to bring freedom and liberty to people all around us.

1 John 2:20 says, "YOU have an anointing from the Holy One." The Spirit of the Lord has anointed you to bring deliverance and freedom to those who are bound and held captive by the enemy.

God's presence and authority go hand in hand, so because of the anointing, you also have authority to break yokes of bondages and set people free!

Another translation of Isaiah 27:10 (NIV) says, "In that day their burden will be lifted from your shoulders, their yoke from your neck; the yoke will be broken because you have grown so fat."

In other words, the yoke, like the burden, will be taken away from Israel; that yoke itself will snap from the pressure of his fat strong neck against it. God is saying, I will strengthen the Israelites, and the yoke that Assyria tries to put on them will not fit. They will try to put their yoke upon you, but it will break because of the strength in your necks. And God will do the same for you!

Because of the finished work of Jesus on the cross, we never have to bear the heavy weight of our sins. He took all of our mistakes, our failures, our pain, and our shame and defeated it all on the cross so that we could live free!

Imagine a yoke tied around the neck of an animal. When that animal fattens and increases in size, it means that the yoke can no longer hold it. It has been so well-fed and becomes so large that it breaks out of its yoke.

You have the same Holy Spirit anointing as Christ had, and as you spend time in God's presence, growing in His word, and allowing Him to work through you, the anointing on your life will begin to grow 'fat'. You will get to a point where certain yokes simply start to break off because they can no longer hold you. As you grow in your walk with God, the fatness of the oil of the Holy Spirit will break yokes off of you because of the anointing!

Galatians 5:1 (NKJV) says, "Stand fast therefore in the liberty by which Christ has made us free, and do not be entangled again with a yoke of bondage."

You don't have to let the devil entangle you because you have the power of the anointing that will break every yoke of bondage. Because of the anointing, we can be delivered from fear, doubt, and oppression, and never be in bondage again!

Because of the finished work of Jesus on the cross, we never have to bear the heavy weight of our sins. He took all of our mistakes, our failures, our pain, and our shame and defeated it all on the cross so that we could live free!

Now, instead of being weighed down by our burdens, Jesus calls us to lay them down and come to Him. Matthew 11:28-30 (NKJV) says, "Come to Me, all you who labor and are heavy laden, and I will give you rest. Take My yoke upon you and learn from Me, for I am gentle and lowly in heart, and you will find rest for your souls. For My yoke is easy and My burden is light."

My prayer is that as you finish reading this book, I hope that you've been able to see a little of yourself in each

Scan to download the song from this chapter.

chapter and I pray that the stories in these pages have made your burden lighter. I hope that you have been encouraged and impacted in ways that you will remember. I hope that you've cried a little, laughed a lot, and were encouraged by a few of my life experiences.

Your journey of pursuing His presence is just beginning. I encourage you to spend time every day reading God's word and worshiping in His presence, and as you do, I believe you will break free of every burden the enemy has put on you and never be in bondage again in Jesus name! I pray that you bring all your worries and cares and lay them down at the feet of Jesus and allow His anointing—the burden-removing, yoke-destroying power of God—to transform you in His presence.

I'd like to end this book by praying for you and as I pray, release every situation that you are worried about and lay all of your burdens down at the feet of Jesus.

MY PRAYER FOR YOU:

May the presence of the Holy Spirit and His anointing empower you as you continue to live a life in pursuit of Jesus. I pray that you would become more aware of God's presence everyday as you spend time in the presence of the Holy Spirit. I pray you will resist the enemy and live in freedom from every yoke and bondage in Jesus' Name! I pray that the burden-removing, yoke-destroying power of God will empower you to walk in the anointing that is on your life. I ask the Holy Spirit to stir up and activate every gift and ability that God has given you, to heal the brokenhearted, proclaim freedom to the captives, and bring liberty to those who are oppressed. You are anointed by the Holy Spirit, and you are His agent to bring freedom and liberty to people all around you! . . . In Jesus' name, amen!

ABOUT THE AUTHOR

Martha Munizzi is a GRAMMY®, Dove®, and Stellar® Award-winning singer-songwriter, pastor, and recording artist, and is considered one of the pioneers of cross-cultural praise and worship music.

Martha has an infectious love for life, a deep love for people, and a zealous love for God's House. Her passion is to help build the church worldwide, see people reach their full potential, and develop and strengthen leaders.

Martha, along with her husband, Dan, and their three children, reside in Orlando, Florida, and are the founders and lead pastors of EpicLife Church in Winter Park, Florida where they both serve as co-pastors.

FOR BOOKING INFO CONTACT US AT:

Martha Munizzi Ministries
P.O. Box 2587
Goldenrod, FL 32733
407-834-5620
booking@marthamunizzi.com

FIND MARTHA AT

🌐 MARTHAMUNIZZI.COM/

📷 WWW.INSTAGRAM.COM/MARTHAMUNIZZI/

📘 WWW.FACEBOOK.COM/MARTHAMUNIZZIFANPAGE

🐦 TWITTER.COM/MARTHAMUNIZZI

▶️ WWW.YOUTUBE.COM/@MARTHAMUNIZZI

CPSIA information can be obtained
at www.ICGtesting.com
Printed in the USA
BVHW051251060623
665472BV00013B/1087